Ivan Sent Me

Ivan Sent Me

A True Story of How Dedication to Duty Solved the Murder of an Innocent Young Woman

By Patrick Burns

JEBWizard Publishing

Books with Character

JEBWizard Publishing
Books with Character

TABLE OF CONTENTS

"Three things cannot long be hidden, the sun, the moon, and the truth."

Buddha

For my children, Kaity and Patrick.

Patrick Burns

Prologue

A charismatic, clever, and brutal young Russian Mobster had gotten away with murder.

With a rock-solid alibi in place, he'd sent two of his hired assassins to brutally kill an innocent young mother. "When you slit her throat, make sure you tell her Ivan Sent You" were his instructions. And that is exactly what they told her when they killed her. It was the last words she would ever hear as her toddler son played in the next room.

And as planned, at the time of her death, Ivan was safely hundreds of miles away, back at his home in rural Amish Country Pennsylvania. His alibi was air-tight and it had worked perfectly. It kept investigators at bay for several years. The only clue left behind by her assassins was a small blood trace. It contained the killer's DNA. It was found on the murder weapon, left by the killers at the scene. One of them had accidentally cut his own hand while slitting the victim's throat.

Patrick Burns

But the DNA was useless to investigators without identifying an individual to match it to. And that seemed impossible. That's because it did not match the DNA of their only suspect, Ivan Teleguz. So the murder became a cold case for three years, and it seemed it would go unsolved indefinitely.

But Ivan was not simply a murderer. He was also a trafficker of drugs, stolen cars, and guns. And his luck began to change when some of his illegal weapons began turning up on the streets 200 miles away, in Springfield, Massachusetts.

That's when an ATF Agent began tracing them, seeking their source. From there, it was only a matter of time before that trail led him to the hired assassins and then to Ivan.

Ivan Sent Me

1   *Cornfields and Killers*

It seemed like any other warm sunny day in picturesque Amish Country, set in rural Lancaster, Pennsylvania. At mid-day, a one-horse buggy trotted slowly along the edge of an otherwise empty two-lane highway. The sound of clip-clopping from the horse's shoes could be heard as they hit the asphalt. Each side of the road's dirt shoulders was flanked by countless acres of farmlands, an almost endless sea of cornfields, all running to the Blue Mountains off on the distant horizon.

Along the roadside, every dozen miles, there were small wooden fruit stands loaded with fresh soybeans, tomatoes, and corn. Giant billboards for tours of the Amish Country loomed above some of the stands. Other billboards touted replicas of dinosaurs to promote a nearby theme park.

A white-bearded driver sat in the buggy, tugging on thick leather reins. His white shirt, black top hat, and dark-colored trousers were the standard local Amish attire.

As the carriage passed by mile marker 103, an American flag waved above the cornfield 100 yards off to the right. Below it, a small, red-brick building served as Pennsylvania State Police's only outpost. Inside it, the three-man skeleton crew was usually more than enough manpower to handle the routine business for such a sleepy farming town.

While the buggy continued to pass, Corporal Ray Guth was just returning to the station. In his mid-forties and the senior officer assigned to the duty station, he pulled his sparkling clean patrol car into the "officer in charge" slot. He stepped out of his cruiser wearing a well-starched uniform. His appearance was spotless, from his head down to his spit-polished boots. He ascended the short cement staircase carrying a paper lunch bag in one hand and toting a Weatherby.308 bolt action deer rifle slung over his shoulder.

A mile further down the road, the horse and buggy approached another gravel side road, also off to the right. A giant green dinosaur replica marked the corner. A rundown barn and dilapidated house were set about a half-mile from the highway. Like everything else in the area, the two buildings are surrounded by thick cornfields.

But the original farmers moved out long ago, and a Russian immigrant family moved in. Their relocation was arranged by a local Mennonite church group. Well-intentioned though they were, the Mennonite leaders eventually learned bringing this family into Lancaster was a big mistake, like allowing a wolf into their hen house.

Patrick Burns

With the farmers gone, so were all the usual implements. The tillers, rakes, and backhoes replaced with tools for a new business -- trafficking in weapons, stolen cars, and drugs.

It had distribution points reaching from coast to coast. A late-model Honda rested in one corner. Its wheels were gone, and it was propped up on cement blocks. One door was also missing. A rainbow of electric wires hung out of a slot in the dashboard where a stereo once fit. Under the windshield, its serial number /VIN was also missing. An unplugged grinding machine sat on the hood, with other tools for disassembly nearby.

In the center of the room, directly below a single dangling bare light bulb, three young men, all in their 20's, talked among themselves as they huddled around an old wooden workbench. The day's work in process was spread out on a wooden table. Parts of a disassembled AK-47 were neatly laid out in order of disassembly. A hand-held grinding machine and a small bottle of "Blue Wonder" are nearby.

Blue Wonder is a gun-bluing liquid used by gun manufacturers to give the silver-colored, bare metal of their firearms a shiny bluish color/finish. It's also sold at retail outlets, used by consumers who want to touch up scratches on their purchased guns. Professional gun traffickers use the product to retouch sections of firearms where they've altered or removed the serial numbers. Obliterating the identifying numbers stifles any future tracing by law enforcement.

After the grinding off of a serial number, the underlying silver-colored bare metal remains exposed. But when a professional gun trafficker adds a layer of gun blue over the bare steel, it restores the gun's original appearance.

As the two men stood on one side of the table attaching the barrel to the weapon's magazine assembly, the short Russian man on the other side of the table looked down at his watch.

"Okay. Time to stop," he said. "We need to go!"

The men laid down the tools as he continued.

"I have another job for you," Ivan Teleguz said.

It was his house, barn, and operation.

*****

The men put away their tools, lit cigarettes, and followed him out to the adjacent dirt parking lot. He locked the barn door behind them. He then ordered them into the passenger side of his pickup truck and fired up the engine. As he shifted into gear, his passengers, two young men, one white and one black, hopped in.

Patrick Burns

"Ed, you ride bitch," the white guy said as he nudged the young, pretty-boy-faced black man into the middle of the bench seat.

Edward Gilkes, a petty thief at best, was in his mid-20's. He was the low man in this crew and knew he was getting in over his head as he sheepishly complied.

Moments later, their truck rumbled down the dirt road and onto the two-lane highway, passing the horse and buggy still clip-clopping along. Minutes later, the truck approached Interstate 81, and Ivan turned it onto the entrance ramp for the southbound lane.

"When we get there, I'll show you her apartment," Teleguz said as he accelerated the truck to the top of the ramp.

"Whose apartment?" Ed asked.

"A woman," he replied as he merges his pickup in with the southbound traffic, "It doesn't matter who she is. She's my ex-girlfriend."

"You're going to pay her a visit for me and deliver a message."

The Russian handed each man a $1,000 wad of cash from his pocket. Each packet of ten $100 bills was bound by a rubber band.

*****

As the truck with the three men continued south on the long, three-hour drive, Corporal Guth entered the State Police station's front lobby. He unsnapped his two-way radio from his belt and handed it to the young officer behind the desk.

"Good morning, boss. Goin' deer hunting again?" He smiled while looking at the Weatherby.308 over Guth's shoulder.

"Charge it please, Billy. And good morning. Anything come in?"

Billy slipped the radio into an open slot in the bank of chargers behind the service desk. The fit young trooper went back to wiping down his work area and filing a few crime reports. A training manual was kept nearby for reading during his lunch breaks.

"Actually, yes, sir. We had another incident. A robbery." Billy retrieved an incident report from the countertop and handed it to Guth.

"Let me guess. Someone saw a green pickup truck in the area?"

"Yep. You guessed it."

Guth continued further into the rear of the small station. He settled in at his desk and tucked his lunch bag into a drawer. Then he laid the Weatherby.308 onto the desktop.

Patrick Burns

The only other item on the spotless desk was a small, framed picture of himself wearing an orange hunting vest and kneeling down in a field. In front of him was a dead 12-point buck.

"Damn it!" Guth muttered under his breath as he examined a small scratch on the rifle's barrel.

He retrieved a small plastic gun cleaning kit from the top drawer, removing a small bottle of Blue Wonder. His rifle, like every other aspect of his life, was meticulously maintained. He carefully leaned inward, close to the gun, focusing on the hairline, almost invisible scratch. Using the small applicator brush, he delicately applied a liquid bluing solution to the blemish. One drop was all it needed.

"*Done*," he thought to himself after blowing gently on the liquid to help it dry. And with that task finished, he sat back and returned to his investigative work.

First, he read the previous night's incident report. A local convenience store was robbed, and the report laid out the details. The clerk was approached by an armed man wearing a ski mask. Although the suspect wore a disguise and gloves, the clerk said he saw some skin color around the mouth portion under the suspect's mask. The gunman was white. The clerk also mentioned that the robber had an unusual foreign-sounding accent.

Guth smiled, then retrieved a file folder from the top draw of his desk. The heading on it read: "Unsolved

Armed Robberies 2001." He flipped open to the section labeled: "Russians/Ivan Teleguz."

Stapled on its cover, Guth first examined a picture of a dark green pickup truck, parked in front of a dilapidated wooden barn and an old farmhouse. Standing next to the truck was a short, muscular Russian in his 20's with a boyish-looking face but sinister eyes. He was wearing a T-shirt and looking straight into the camera. Guth recalled the day he took that picture. It was a day after one of the recent armed robberies.

After learning that Ivan's truck matched the possible getaway vehicle's description, Guth decided to stake-out the barn. Many more surveillances followed after that day, so this photo was just one of many. But despite his relentless efforts, so far, nothing had come of it. He had no evidence/charges against the Russian suspect.

Guth put the folder away while recalling how surprised he was to see the level of arrogance in such a young man. Despite seeing a marked State Police cruiser parked literally at his doorstep, just one day after having committed an armed robbery, Teleguz appeared callous to his presence.

During the day, the insolent thief even paused as he crossed the yard to look directly at him, almost taunting Guth to snap the photo.

Patrick Burns

Ray laid down the case file, removed a photo from it, and held it up to the light. Suddenly he spotted something he hadn't' noticed before -- something shiny hanging on the barn door. He looked closer. The old, dilapidated barn seemed all but falling apart. Yet, on its door, something was hung that looked like a large, shiny expensive padlock.

"Find anything, boss?" Billy asked as he entered the room.

"Billy, why would Teleguz need such an expensive lock on an old barn door?

"I don't know."

"I'll tell you what, Bill. I'd love to see inside that barn."

"Maybe we could just go over there and ask to look around? You know, get a Consent Search?"

"That's a great idea, Bill. But he'd never go for it. And we simply don't have enough evidence to establish probable cause. A judge would never approve a search warrant based simply on the fact that he owns a green truck similar to the one always appearing in the vicinity of robberies. So for now, we'll have to just keep working, and waiting, and hoping for a break."

*****

As the work continued in Lancaster, a couple hundred miles south, in Harrisonburg, Virginia, the residential street was quiet. The sun was just setting over one of the apartment buildings.

"Dinner's almost ready, hun," Stephanie Sipe's neighbor said as her husband grabbed a half-smoked cigarette butt from the ashtray and headed toward their balcony door.

"I'll be just a minute," he replied while stepping through the glass door and onto the rickety wooden balcony.

As he fired up the half-burned cigarette butt, saved from earlier in the day, he took a good long drag, inhaling a lung-full of relaxing smoke. It's was a beautiful and warm July evening. As usual, the street was empty and quiet, except for an occasional siren heard in the distance, coming from downtown Harrisonburg. He enjoyed the few moments before dinner.

"Five minutes!" his wife reminded him through the door opening.

He took a final puff on the cigarette butt. As he did, he had a feeling of being watched. He scanned the street, looking for anything unusual, and his eyes stopped on a dark-colored truck across the street.

It was parked in the shadow of a giant oak tree, and there appeared to be three figures inside the cab. *"Are they watching me?"* he wondered, pausing a moment before going back inside. Just then, one of the silhouetted figures lit a cigarette. For an instant, he could vaguely see their faces.

"I'm coming." The man re-entered the apartment and closed the glass door behind himself. As he flipped the latch on the lock, he froze for an instant as the thought hit him. For some reason, the truck looked familiar.

One floor up, the crackling sound of splattering grease could be heard as the aroma of sizzling hotdogs filled the room. Stephanie Sipe tended them with a spatula as tears ran down her cheeks.

A few feet away, seated behind her at an old, laminated table, her two-year-old son, Zachary, smiled as he waits for dinner. But then the little blonde-haired toddler noticed her tears.

"Why are you crying, mommy? What's wrong?"

"Tears of joy, honey. Happy tears."

Next to the stove was a picture of her and her son seated on Santa's lap, taken the previous Christmas. Stephanie looked young and beautiful with long, light brown hair. Zachary seemed as happy as ever sitting with her.

Next to the picture was a stack of unpaid bills. On top was the day's mail, including an opened envelope from the Probate Court. It stated that she had been awarded child support money from the boy's estranged father, Ivan Teleguz.

"Tears of joy, Zachary! Everything will be fine now, my love," she said as she scooped a lump of macaroni and cheese onto his plate next to the hotdog slices.

Just then, the phone rang.

"Eat your dinner, honey. Grandma is calling. She calls to ask about you every day. She loves you."

Stephanie took the phone call. "Mom, I'll call you later. I'm just getting Zachary ready for bed."

The men down on the street continued to watch her window.

"That's her. In the second-floor window," Teleguz told his two men, pointing to his ex-girlfriend as she passed the lit window.

Michael Hetrick opened his door to exit the truck, eager to do the job. The muscular thug's face was blank, free of emotion. He was wearing a dark-colored T-shirt to conceal himself in the shadows and a baseball cap to hide his appearance. Like Ivan, Hetrick was cold-blooded and ruthless, with no second thoughts about taking a life for the right price.

Patrick Burns

"Hey! Close the door!" Teleguz scolded him. "Not now. I'll drop you off around the corner. I can't be seen here, you idiot!"

"Got it," Hetrick said as he closed the door.

Teleguz started the engine and drove to the end of the neighborhood street. He flipped on the headlights and headed to a nearby parking lot.

"First, I'll drop you off around the corner," he told Hetrick. "And then I need time to get back to Lancaster before you go in."

"Why?" Hetrick asked.

"I need to have an alibi, you idiot."

Driving about a mile away, Teleguz pulled his pickup truck to the unlit end of a nearby parking lot. He shut off the headlights and unscrewed the dome light. Turning to face the men, he reinforced his instructions.

"Wait here for three hours," he ordered. "I need three hours to drive back to Lancaster for my alibi. I'll have witnesses there who will say they saw me there at the time you visit her. That way, I'll prove I was hundreds of miles away, in Lancaster.

"Sure, Ivan. Whatever you say," Gilkes replied nervously.

"After three hours, you can walk back to her apartment. One of you stay outside as the lookout and watch for the cops, and the other goes in. After you finish, take a bus back to Pennsylvania. Buses don't keep records of who travels on them."

"Ivan, I told you before," Gilkes said while trying to steady his hand to light another cigarette. "You guys know me; I'm just a thief."

Sweat was visibly beading up on his temples.

"Shut up, Ed. You'll stay outside. Michael will go in," Teleguz handed a six-inch knife to Michael.

Hetrick silently tucked it into the back of his pants.

Teleguz knew that a gunshot could be heard by her neighbors. That might create potential witnesses, and he was too savvy to make that mistake. But a knife was silent, and as long was Hetrick wiped off the handle for his fingerprints, it couldn't be traced like a gun.

He also realized that a gun would leave a bullet behind. Investigators would eventually find her body and do an autopsy. Once a bullet is recovered, it can be matched to the murder weapon. Once a murder weapon was identified, it would have serial numbers. At that point, it could be traced to the purchaser and eventually to the killer. But a knife left no such evidence behind.

As the two men begin to exit the truck, Ivan reminded them,

Patrick Burns

"Hey! When you slit her throat, tell her IVAN SENT ME!"

2   *Ivan Sent Me*

Hours later, back at the apartment, Stephanie continued with her nightly routine. She ran a bath for the toddler. Soon the boy was smiling in the rising tub water, surrounded by his floating toys. She smiled at seeing how happy her son was, knowing that she could finally give him everything he needed thanks to the recent court order. Again, her eyes filled with tears of happiness.

The phone rang.

"That's grandma, honey. Mommy will be right back."

Stephanie quickly walked to the phone to answer the expected phone call from her mother, then stopped when she heard an unexpected knock at the front door. She unlatched the deadbolt and chain lock.

"Hello, ma'am," a sincere-looking young man said, "Sorry to bother you. My car broke down. Could I use your phone?"

She hesitated for a moment, knowing she was alone in the apartment with the boy. But she was brought up to help people.

16

"Ah, Okay, Come in. The phone's right over here in the kitchen."

As she turned to lead him into the small kitchen, Michael closed the door behind them. His smile fell from his face as he slowly removed the knife from its concealment under his shirt.

The phone rang again, and Stephanie turned to pick it up. As she did, she saw Hetrick raise the knife.

"What are you doing?" she screamed in disbelief.

He closed in. She moved away as he chased her around the kitchen, stabbing at her. Stephanie fought back, holding up her hands in defense as she backed away. But Hetrick continues stabbing at her. Finally, bleeding, in excruciating pain, she was backed into a corner, crying, and pleading for him to stop.

The killer ignored her pleas. He pressed her up against the wall. While holding her throat with his left hand, he uses his right hand and runs the sharp blade across her soft neck.

"Ivan sent me!" he told her as he looked her in the eyes and completed inflicting the fatal slash.

As she fell limp to the floor, and the heat of the moment faded, Michael suddenly became aware of a sharp pain running up his arm.

"Fuck!" Hetrick exclaimed as he dropped the murder weapon onto the kitchen floor, then grabbed his wounded hand to ease the pain and slow the bleeding.

Hetrick forced himself to straighten up and rushed to the bathroom sink to clean his wound. Still in pain, he turned on the water and ran it over his hand for several minutes.

As the water flushed out his wound, and the pain lessens, he sensed something. He looked up in the mirror. In the reflection, over his shoulder, he saw floating toys in a full bathtub. Between them, he spotted a set of tiny eyes watching him.

A living witness.

Ivan never mentioned a small boy, and he gave no instructions as to what to do with him. Hetrick needed to decide. He looked back to the kitchen where the knife was sitting in a pool of blood, then at the bathtub. The faucet was still turned on and running. The water continued to rise.

He knew that if he did nothing, there would be no witnesses left behind. It wouldn't take long for the water level to get too deep for the toddler to keep his head above water, and the problem would be solved on its own.

But killing the boy was not part of the deal. Hetrick pondered his options as he casually turned off the sink water and took a few minutes to bandage his wound. He then turned toward the boy and reached into the tub. As the boy looked up at him, he simply shut off the faucet and opened the drain. With that done, Hetrick straightened up, looked around, cupped his wounded hand, and silently exited the apartment. Moments later, he disappeared back into the shadows.

With Stephanie dead, the only sound in the apartment was splashing as the boy tried to keep his head above water.

Later, Stephanie's mother called again to check on her daughter and grandson. The phone went unanswered, so the next morning, she called again. Still no response.

On the morning of July 23, 2001, two of Stephanie's neighbors heard screams and found Stephanie's mother standing over her daughter's body.

"Oh, my God! No! Oh my God!" she screamed, in shock, frozen, crying, and wailing.

"Stay here!" said Sonny Rich, one of the neighbors, after calling the police on his cell phone. He went inside, looking for the boy.

The other neighbor, Mr. Moore, also entered the apartment. He noticed the bathroom door was closed and heard faint crying coming from inside. He went inside and found Zachary.

Within minutes, sirens could be heard in the distance. Uniformed officers leaped out of their cars and secured the scene. One draped yellow "POLICE LINE" tape on the apartment door entrance and the door to the victim's apartment. At the same time, other officers gathered the neighbors for witness statements.

Inside the kitchen and bathroom of Stephanie's apartment, the evidence team went to work. All were wearing matching blue windbreakers and white rubber gloves, and some had unpacked their cameras. Others began to lay out orange, sequentially numbered plastic cones or broke out note pads, evidence bags, and other trade tools.

The photographer took a picture of blood splatter on the bathroom sink. Another officer marked it with a numbered cone. The photographer snapped off another shot that included the marker and then got several other angles of the sink.

Soon, other cones marked various locations on the floor. Numbered yellow sticky pads were used to mark areas on the walls and cupboards where blood splatter traces are visible. As the team worked, an artist stood off to one side of the room, sketching a diagram of the overall scene. In it, he carefully outlined the location and angle of the knife lying on the floor. It lay in the edge of the pool of blood, and visible on its blade and handle was more blood.

Patrick Burns

As the police photographer finished her work, the coroner arrived to retrieve the body, followed by Harrisonburg Detective Kevin Whitfield, a seasoned, methodical investigator. Without a word, he carefully took his initial walk-through of the scene. The home didn't seem to have been "tossed." There were no signs of forced entry. Robbery didn't seem to have been the motive. Whitfield also noted that the victim was fully clothed, and it didn't appear that she was raped. So what was the motive, he wondered?

Whitfield then sat down with the first witness on the scene, Stephanie's mother, who was still sobbing and visibly in shock.

"Ma'am, do you know if your daughter had any enemies? Anyone you think that may have done this?"

"Everyone loved her," she sobbed. "She was even kind to strangers," she replied while fighting more tears and gasping for air.

"I see. So then can I ask you, why did you come to Stephanie's apartment today? Did something happen?"

"My daughter calls me every day. I hadn't heard from her in three days. So I came to see what was wrong. My God," she sobbed. "I can't believe this. I told her that man was no good!"

"Wait. Wait. …What man? Who?"

"Zachary's father! Ivan Teleguz. He did this; I know it. He told her not to ask for child support. But she had no choice. She needed to take care of my grandson!" she replied, then broke into tears again.

Whitfield jotted down the name of Ivan Teleguz.

"Where can I find him?"

"I don't know. I think he lives in Lancaster. That's all I know," she replied as she broke down again.

"Lancaster, Pennsylvania?"

"Yes. Yes."

"Thank you, ma'am. I'm sorry for your loss. We will do everything we can."

The neighbors, including Rich, were nearby as Whitfield began his second interview with Rich. He handed another officer the page from his notepad with Teleguz's name on it. The officer needed no explanation. Without a word, he quickly departed the room to search the databases for an address and description for their new prime—and only—suspect.

Meanwhile, the evidence technicians continued their tedious work of documenting the scene, dusting the suspected murder weapon for fingerprints, and taking blood samples from various locations.

Patrick Burns

"That one from the sink area goes to the lab first," Whitfield yelled as he saw a crime scene tech taking an evidence bag from the bathroom area.

Turning his attention back to the witness, he asked, "Did you see anyone suspicious that night, the evening of the 21st?"

"Yes," Rich said. "I did. I was on my balcony, smoking a cigarette. And I saw a man walking away from the building that night. It must have been him."

Whitfield retrieved a photo recovered from the apartment. It's a picture of the victim and a rough-looking, short man.

"Was this the man you saw leaving the apartment at the time of the murder?" Whitfield asked while holding up a picture of Ivan Teleguz.

"I think so," Rich said.

"You *think* so?" You're not sure?"

"It was dark. I can't be positive."

"Thank you very much," Whitfield said, disappointed that the witness could not positively ID Ivan Teleguz at the scene.

An officer rushed into the room. "We found his address. It's a farmhouse in Lancaster, Pennsylvania."

"Beautiful! Please contact the Pennsylvania State Police for that area. Ask them to assign someone to join me tomorrow. I'm gonna pay a little visit to Ivan Teleguz."

Whitfield knew that it would take considerable time before he could expect to get back any results from the forensics. The fingerprint samples could take a few days; the blood analysis would take much longer. But he couldn't wait that long. Timing is especially critical at this stage of an investigation. He needed to lock-in witness testimony before memories faded. He couldn't afford to delay interviewing his prime and only suspect as he waited for the lab work to be completed. He needed to find Teleguz ASAP and look for any other potential witnesses that may help put the Russian at the scene when Stephanie was murdered.

*****

Early the next morning, on July 24, 2001, Whitfield was on his way. Holding the steering wheel with one hand, he sipped on a giant-sized coffee with his other.

After 200 miles of Interstate 81, he spotted the exit for Lancaster, PA, leading to a quiet two-lane highway. The road's dirt shoulders were flanked by countless acres of farmlands, with the majestic Blue Ridge Mountains off in the distance.

Moments later, the detective recognized his destination. An American flag waved in the breeze at the end of a short dirt road.

After the usual introductions, Detective Whitfield and Corporal Guth reviewed the case.

"As I told you on the phone, we only have one suspect, one man with a known motive to kill Ms. Sipe. He's living in your area. His name is Ivan Teleguz," Whitfield explained.

"I know exactly who that is. Teleguz is my prime suspect in every violent crime I've investigated since I arrived here in Lancaster. I've got open cases on armed robberies, car thefts, drug trafficking. All trails lead to him… And now he's done a murder. I wish I could say I was surprised. Anyway, I'm happy to do whatever I can do to help. What do you need, Detective?"

"I'd like you to accompany me to his house and see if we can get him to talk. We want to at least place him at the scene."

"I know this guy. He's young. But he's as cold-blooded as any criminal I've ever come across. He won't cooperate. I'm sure of that."

"Well, we'll tell him we know he is the only person in the world who has a motive to kill her. It seems he wanted her dead because he was ordered to pay her $119 per week in child support for their son Zachary.

And we'll also tell him that we found two blood types at the scene. Once the lab results come in, we'll be able to prove the blood on the murder weapon and on the sink was his. Then it's game over."

"Okay, sounds like a plan. Let's go see Teleguz. It's a short drive to his farmhouse."

Guth parked his cruiser in front of the barn door when they arrived. The door was open. He briefly glanced around the area, then entered the dimly lit barn. It seemed utterly empty. With nothing to see after looking around for a moment, he turned to follow Whitfield toward the house. As he did, his eyes caught on a single ray of sunlight passing through a gap in the barn wall. It was falling onto the only item remaining on the wooden workbench, a small bottle. He instantly recognized it as gun blue. *Why would Teleguz need gun blue liquid,* he wondered?

They entered the house to find Teleguz sitting at a table as if he'd expected them. An elderly woman looked at them like intruders.

"Mr. Teleguz, where were you on the evening of July 21?" Whitfield asked.

"I was here at home with my mom. Go ahead. Ask her. She's right behind you."

He looked at his mother standing nearby, watching.

Patrick Burns

She nodded affirmatively.

"Do you know this woman?" Whitfield asked Teleguz as he held up a picture of Stephanie and young Zachary. In the photo, they were both smiling and sitting on the lap of a store Santa Claus.

"Of course, I know her. That's my son and my ex-girlfriend. Is it a crime if I know her? Are you going to arrest me?"

Teleguz gave the two officers a disdainful smile.

"Is this a joke?" Whitfield asked as he next held up a photo from the crime scene. It was a picture of Stephanie lying dead on the floor with her throat cut. He then held up an image of a sink with blood on it. Finally, he showed Ivan a photo of the murder weapon.

"So what? That's got nothing to do with me. Like I said, I was here, and I can prove it. You've got nothing."

"Nothing?" Whitfield replied, his anger building. "Guess what, asshole? The blood on the sink is too far from the body. It cannot have all come from the victim. I think some of it's yours."

"I told you. Are you stupid? I wasn't there!"

"You WERE there. So let's just get this over with now. Admit it."

"You are full of shit, cop. In fact, if you don't have an arrest warrant, get out of my house!"

"Sure, Ivan, we'll leave for now. But as soon as the lab report comes in, we'll be back. By the way, Virginia has the death penalty. So I'll be looking forward to watching you on your walk down death row!"

As they pulled away in the police cruiser, Teleguz was on the front porch smiling and waving.

"He sure looks like he knows something that we don't know," Guth said as they drove back to the station.

"We'll see about that. His alibi won't hold up," Whitfield predicted.

3   *Welcome to Springfield*

Months later, the phone on Guth's desk rang.

"Hi Ray, it's me, Whitfield in Harrisonburg. I have good news. We got the lab report back."

"Can we arrest him now?"

"No. I don't have an arrest warrant yet. But I do have a search warrant."

"For the house?"

"It's for Ivan's DNA. The lab report proves that the blood found on the sink didn't belong to the victim. Therefore it had to come from the killer. So that's why I'm calling. I have a search warrant to take a DNA sample from our friend, Ivan Teleguz. Then we can see if it matches the sample from the sink."

"OK. Just let me know when you are coming, and I'll join you. I'll be glad to assist. We need to get this monster off the street before he kills someone else."

A few days later, Guth and Whitfield are back at the farmhouse. Guth witnessed the process as Whitfield cut a hair sample from Teleguz. Then Whitfield took a swab and rubbed it inside of Teleguz's cheeks, collecting saliva. When they finished, Teleguz smirked and mocked the officers yet again.

"Enjoy yourself now, Ivan," Whitfield said. "This right here," he said while holding up the plastic dish with the samples in it, "is going to get you the death penalty."

"If you're done, get the fuck out of my house... You people are clowns."

"Sure. Ivan," Guth said. "But we'll be back, smart ass!"

Around the same time the hair and saliva samples were on the way to the lab, I was just starting at my new job as a Special Agent for the Bureau of Alcohol, Tobacco, and Firearms. It was actually my third try at finding a career that was the right fit.

After serving three years in the U.S. Marines and getting honorably discharged in 1979, I completed a Bachelor of Science Degree program at a local university. My major was in accounting. I later met the requirements to become a certified public accountant.

That career didn't last long – I found little job satisfaction in spending my days counting other people's money. So I started a new career, taking a position as a Special Agent with the U.S. Treasury Department.

Initially, working for the IRS-CID seemed my dream job. I planned on following in the footsteps of men like Elliot Ness, chasing dangerous federal criminals by using financial crime laws as my tools. My first few years on the job were that—exciting and satisfying—just what I'd hoped for. I aggressively opened dozens of investigations of high-level mobsters and international money launderers.

But although the cases were successful in court and successful as far as I was concerned, they weren't deemed successful as far as the IRS upper management was concerned. The IRS Headquarters muckety-mucks needed tax dollar "statistics" if they wanted to continue getting their fat bonuses.

It took time, but I eventually realized that the IRS-CID didn't operate as I'd hoped. Unlike what I saw portrayed in some Hollywood movies—treasury agents crashing through doors, shotguns in-hand—the IRS bosses had no stomach for us chasing real criminals.

Real criminals were challenging targets. They were expensive to pursue and dangerous to encounter. Most importantly, they didn't pay taxes. Working in the IRS bowels in Washington, D.C., the executives wanted no part of that. They cared exclusively about collecting taxes and showing impressive statistics to the budget committees.

The best way for them to do that—and produce the statistical reports that led to their bonuses—was by pursuing only the easiest of targets, those without guns and smart attorneys.

They seemed to have worked out a process for new hires. During a rookie agent's first few years, they give the young, aggressive guys and women more leeway. They don't want to crush their enthusiasm too quickly. The plan is to do it gradually, so the agents don't even notice it. Using micromanagement tactics that would demoralize even the best, they ground agent enthusiasm into dust.

For most agents, that is.

But when the honeymoon was over, and it was time to entirely pull in the reins, they did just that. They'd strongly encourage agents to only pursue the "right" targets.

In my case, when I didn't get the subtle hints, they eventually just called me onto the carpet directly. I was told straight out, so there was no misunderstanding. I'd no longer be allowed to pursue dangerous criminals in organizations such as La Cosa Nostra or the Colombian drug cartels.

Going forward, I'd be allowed only to pursue income tax cases against people with *legal income sources*. And I was further informed that if I couldn't be content with pursuing targets like plumbers and waitresses, I should seek employment elsewhere.

Patrick Burns

So that is what I did in the spring of 2000. I started over again in my career, hoping this third try was, as they say, the charm.

I looked around at other federal law enforcement agencies. This was a few years after ATF had gotten into the infamous shoot-out at the Branch Dravidian Compound in Waco, TX. Four agents were killed that day, and many more were injured in ATFs' most publicized gunfight.

I found that more ATF agents had been killed in the line of duty over the years than all other agencies combined. I didn't want to become the next in line for that. But I did want to go after America's most dangerous criminals. If I was going to spend my life in this line of work, why not go after the worst of the worst?

Yet that meant I needed to go back to rookie agent training at the Federal Law Enforcement Training Academy (F.L.E.T.C). I needed to get specialized weapons training. After spending several long months in blistering, black fly-infested Glynco, GA, struggling to keep up with classmates who were almost half my age, I finally graduated and received my initial assignment.

Thus, it was 2001, and I was at my first post of duty, Springfield, Massachusetts. Although it was hundreds of miles away from Teleguz in Lancaster, PA, it would seem unlikely that our paths would ever cross. But it's a small world, and anything was possible.

That's because if there's one certainty about career criminals, they'll always continue to commit additional crimes. That's their Achilles heel. No matter how clever or savvy they are, it's often just a matter of time before they make a mistake. And when that happens, sometimes the person on their trail comes out of nowhere—for example, 200 miles away in Springfield.

When I arrived, I found a city ravaged by gangs and gun violence. It wasn't always that way. Back in its heyday, during the early and mid-1900s, Springfield was known as "The City of Homes" for the abundance of gorgeous affluent Victorian-style mansions that dominated the city. Their wealthy inhabitants owned and worked at the prosperous mills downtown. It appealed to many industries due to its location—right on the Connecticut River, 150 miles from New York City, and 100 miles from Boston.

But by 2001, most mills had closed. The jobs were gone. Most of the gorgeous mansions had fallen into disrepair. Some were burned down, others were abandoned and covered with gang graffiti. Of those that remained, some were chopped up into multi-units for low-income housing.

Along with the city's decline came gangs, drugs, guns, and violence.

The good news was there was plenty of work to do as an ATF agent. But despite all the work to be done, the office maintained only a skeleton crew. When I began, it was myself and one other agent, my on-the-job instructor. We enforced the federal gun and explosive laws for the entire western half of Massachusetts. Our area of responsibility went from Sturbridge to the west end of the state near Albany, NY.

If that wasn't challenging enough, my instructor was about to be transferred to the Federal Law Enforcement Training Academy (F.L.E.T.C.) in southern Georgia. So our two-man office was soon to become a one-man office.

That made it critical to keep good working relationships with the other federal, state, and local agencies. One way to do that was to participate in the FBI's Gang Task Force.

I was accepted and included in an operation planned for late one morning. My assignment was to be on the arrest team. But just as I was about to head out, I ran into a brief, unexpected delay. There'd been a death in my family. It was Spike, my son's guinea pig.

At 8:00 a.m., Patrick Jr. and I were standing in the corner of our small backyard, directly under the shade of a large pine tree. We took a moment to look down at the shallow grave we'd just finished digging. Patrick found an appropriate rock to serve as a tombstone. Now it was time to take a moment to say a few last words about the recently deceased.

My daughter was in the house, modeling her new cheerleading uniform while we completed the ceremony. My wife was also in the house, likely updating her unabridged, extensive list of my shortcomings.

"Do you have anything you want to say?" I asked as we both solemnly looked down at the small grave.

"Yes," he replied with an eager yet thoughtful smile.

"Okay, buddy. Go ahead."

"Spike, you were a great guinea pig," he said and then looked up to me.

"Is that it?" I asked.

He nodded, shrugged his shoulders, and replied simply, "Yep."

"Okay then...It's time to get you ready for school, and I need to go to work."

The Task Force's target was a high-level, high-risk drug trafficker. Today's deal was set for late that morning and was set to go down in Springfield's south end. The Task Force leader, FBI Agent Rob Lewis—a former naval officer and seasoned Special Agent—carefully selected the safest possible location he could find. He chose the rear of a private parking lot, set behind a ring of commercial brick buildings. They would serve as a barrier if any shots were fired during the arrest.

The target was a Latin King gang member. He was armed and dangerous. He had explicitly told Rob's informant that he'd been to jail before and would rather die than go back. He vowed to never be taken alive.

Knowing all of that, I expected today would be eventful. I took the final sip of my coffee and checked my watch. It was time to go. But as I walked over to the trunk of my government car to gear up, I heard the glass door opening. I turned to see little Patrick running back out toward me with a stuffed turtle under his arm.

"Dad, can I come with you today to catch bad guys?" he asked as he ran up beside me.

I continued slipping my body armor over my head as I replied. "Not today, buddy."

It was a question he'd asked almost daily.

"Please, please, please," he said, now looking up to me with wide eyes, pleading, not yet in his school uniform, holding a stuffed turtle.

As he stood there, still seemingly undeterred, I retrieved some ammunition from the duffel bag in my car's trunk. As I did, I wondered if I'd made the right decision. I was now forty-two and starting all over.

As I remained standing behind my open car trunk, putting on my body armor and checking my weapon, Patrick begged to join me. As I pulled down the trunk hatch, Patrick rushed forward and tossed his stuffed turtle inside. If *he* couldn't come with me to catch bad guys, at least his turtle would be going along in his place. So, with the turtle in the trunk, I headed to the operational meeting at the Springfield FBI office.

***

When I arrived at the FBI office, many of the teams were already gearing up. Their cars filled the parking spots behind it. The commercial building sat in an industrial section of the city, away from the downtown area and most of our operations. It was beyond the prying eyes of most of the targets in the city.

As the first teams filtered into the office, others were still arriving. A few more had been delayed. They were still finishing a meeting at the Springfield P.D. headquarters, wishing one of their own good luck.

One of their detectives was moving on to the State Police. On his last day as a detective, his colleagues were huddled around his desk on the second-floor detectives' bureau.

The large, open dusty room, filled with a couple dozen World War II-era desks and a few vintage file cabinets, was their home. One window had an unrepaired bullet hole in it, evidently a message from one of their unsatisfied clients. Above the men, the ceiling was covered by white and yellow water-stained, broken drop-ceiling panels. Some were dangling in place, held up with bent clothes hangers. Others were simply missing, exposing the wires and sewage pipes above them.

As the handful of well-wishers looked on, the guest of honor blew out his candles. Along with candles, the cake had an image of a Massachusetts State Police Trooper standing in uniform next to his patrol car. Below it, covering his desk like a tablecloth, the other officers had draped a movie poster of Starsky and Hutch.

"Looks like we need a new poster to hang in the office. No more Starsky and Hutch!" joked one onlooker.

Detective Norman Shink, aka the "Starsky" in the team, a six-foot-six, aggressive, door-kicking brute with a permanent smile on his face, was the guest of honor. His partner, Detective Sean Condon, aka "Hutch," was just as aggressive but more subtle. He stood by smiling and looking on.

It was a bittersweet moment for the two. They'd been a team ever since they entered law enforcement, first working together as prison guards at the local jail. Later they were both accepted onto the P.D. simultaneously and had been partners ever since.

For the following decade, they aggressively worked the streets. Together they had more car chases, foot chases, car crashes, and arrests than most other detectives combined, earning themselves the nicknames Starsky and Hutch.

On the street, they were known by different nicknames. "The gangs will now need to call Sean Salt without Pepper!" one man laughed.

Both men looked older than their years, sporting prematurely gray and white hair. The gangsters on the street called them "Salt and Pepper." Whenever Norm and Sean's cruiser was spotted pulling into gang territories, the warning went out "Salt and Pepper, Salt and Pepper."

Most would flee—on foot, in cars, by any means—as long as it was fast. And that's where the chases and crashes began.

But for now, the two went on their separate ways, and as the party broke up, the remaining Task Force members headed over to the FBI office to catch up on the others. Some were suiting up with radios and weapons, while others continued filtering inside to the briefing room.

*****

A few miles away, in a rough section of the city, where dirt lawns, broken-down cars, barking pit bulls, and chain-link fences were the standard ambiance, their target was also preparing for his meeting later in the day.

With a 9mm pistol tucked into his pants, the disheveled-looking, dark-skinned man, dressed in baggy black-and-gold shorts, and wearing a large gold chain around his neck, exited the back door of a small, dilapidated apartment building.

Walking through the tiny dirt lot, he navigated around several discarded trash bags and broken appliances glancing around at the adjoining backyards. Seeing nothing unusual, he removed the 9 mm pistol from the small of his back.

While continuing toward his vehicle, the man slowly pulled back the slide on the top of the gun. The morning sun sparkled against the brass colored bullet, now exposed as it slips forward into the barrel. With the sound of a click, the round was seated. He then inspected a small, silver-colored section just above the trigger, a spot half the size of a postage stamp, where the serial number used to be.

With everything in order, he tucked the weapon back in his waistband and lit a Swisher Sweet cigar. Glancing around the street for any sign of suspicious cars, he looked for anything that may indicate cops.

Seeing nothing unusual, he hopped into his minivan and reached under the seat to retrieve a baby's diaper bag. He tucked a kilo of cocaine into the bag, now ready for concealed transport to the meet. Satisfied, the gangster smiled as he tossed the empty pack of Swisher Sweets over his right shoulder. It landed in an empty baby's car seat.

With the engine running, he shifted into gear and again scanned the street. All seemed clear. Only the usual broken-down cars on the street and the usual hoodlums gathered in small groups on the nearby front porches. All were preparing to start their day of drinking liter-sized bottles of Colt 45 and smoking blunts while waiting for their crack clients to arrive.

***

On the other end of town, on the second floor of the FBI building, a group of agents, state troopers, local officers, and sheriffs gathered around a conference table in one corner of the building. The room was full. Many were seated; others stood along the walls. FBI Agent Rob Lewis stood at one end of the table as he started the briefing.

Behind him on the wall was a whiteboard with his hand-drawn map on it. It depicted the proposed scene for the day's operation, a deserted parking lot at the end of an alleyway in the south end of town.

Patrick Burns

"To begin, I'd like to introduce today's team members," Lewis said in his usual soft-spoken manner.

He had been on the job for more than a decade. He had quietly worked his way up through the ranks, first as an NCIS Special Agent for the U.S. Navy and later for the FBI. During that entire time, his work-record remained spotless. Now, only halfway through his career, he'd already racked up hundreds of arrests. No one in the room was more respected.

"First of all, I'd like everyone to take a good look at Carlos, our cooperating informant," Lewis said, gesturing toward a rough-looking Hispanic man wearing black and gold clothing, Latin King gang colors.

Carlos smiled, revealing his shiny gold-plated front tooth. He waved and tried to make eye contact with everyone in the room. If things went south, as was often the case in undercover buy-busts, he hoped all the pale faces surrounding him in this room would recognize him, amid the chaos, as one of the good guys.

"Carlos will remain in the van. But I wanted you all to be familiar with him anyway, just in case. Today, Carlos has set up a one-kilo purchase. The target is a Latin King gang member. He's known to be armed and extremely dangerous.

"The meet is set for 10:30 am because we need to finish before the rush-hour crowds start flooding Main Street and before local school kids get out. We can't afford to have any innocent bystanders or children wandering into a potential gunfight. Now, is everyone familiar with the location? It's the parking lot behind the recycling center on Main Street in the south end."

The men and women all nodded, raised a hand, or answered that they were familiar with the location.

"Okay, Carlos and I will be in the back of our undercover van. He'll contact the target. Once we know he's heading our way, Eddie," Lewis pointed to the young Hispanic officer standing near the door, "Eddie will be our eyeball. He'll be posted at the highway exit ramp and alert us when the target's van enters the city."

"10-4, boss," Eddie smiled and nodded.

"And Eddie, I have a special vehicle for you today," Lewis added with a smirk.

"Special?" asked the rookie officer, with a puzzled look.

A few veterans seated around the table laughed, seeming to know the punch line to this inside joke that Eddie was yet to learn.

"Okay. Continuing on," Lewis raised his finger to point to a line in the center of the map. "After Eddie follows the target along Main Street to the alley/entrance of the parking lot, he'll turn the eyeball over to Springfield Officer Mike Chapdelaine.

Patrick Burns

"Chappy will take over the eyeball from there." Lewis nodded to one of the other Springfield plainclothes officers seated at the table.

Chappy raised his hand and briefly glanced around to the others.

"And finally, the arrest team will include, among others, our newest member to the Task Force and our oldest," Lewis looked over at a gray-haired, barrel-chested officer wearing a tattered blue sweater and me. We were seated together at the table.

"Agent Burns is newly assigned to ATF's Springfield office, and Detective Steve Maurangadakis, who I'm sure everyone here knows, has been on the job since forever. I think he patrolled on horseback when he first started." Lewis issued a quick smile.

"Yeah, and that sweater of his has been on the job longer than most of us too!" joked one of his fellow officers.

"But don't try to pronounce his name!" joked another.

"Just call me the Greek," said Maurangadakis as he stroked his long, gray handlebar mustache. He was used to the jokes. It was all between friends.

"So that's it! Once the target enters the alley, the arrest team will move in, and we will snap closed the trap.

"Right behind the arrest vehicle, Drug Enforcement Administration (DEA) agents will follow into the alley and park their car in the middle, closing off the only escape route. Done!"

The group members grabbed their coffees, note pads, and two-way radios from the conference table and stood.

"Thanks, guys. Let's get out there and set up," Lewis said as the group filed out of the conference room.

On our way out, walking through the FBI's sprawling office, we passed dozens of officers and agents dressed in suits and ties working cases such as political corruption, bankruptcy frauds, and other crimes.

The drug unit was easily identified by their attire— loose fitted casual shirts and blue jeans— and activity— stacking drug evidence and counting cash from their most recent seizure. Next to the exit sat a cluster of empty workstations and several cardboard boxes.

"Someone leaving?" I asked the Greek.

"No. Someone is coming, a new guy."

"From where?"

"I heard through the grapevine that he's from Washington, D.C., part of their secret squirrel unit."

"Secret squirrels?"

Patrick Burns

“Yeah, you know,” he paused a moment. “the guys that follow the spies around. They call them secret squirrels because no one knows exactly what they do. They don't even talk to their own people. They're like ghosts.”

*****

Fifteen minutes later, the teams were covertly moving into the south end of town, filtering into the neighborhoods surrounding the planned take-down site.

Inside our silver minivan, the Greek and I slowly advanced along Main Street in heavy traffic, heading toward are our staging site. We'd hide our van behind an abandoned gas station. It's just one block from the alley that we'd need to get to quickly once we get word that the target is coming.

As we continued along Main Street, the Greek shook his head in despair. “Look at this place. It used to be beautiful,” looking out the window and gesturing toward a boarded-up business on the side of the road, covered with graffiti and surrounded with trash.

“Now it's a fucking dump!”

Our vehicle continued along a one-mile section of town formerly known as *Little Italy*.

“This used to go on for ten blocks. It was filled with beautiful Italian restaurants and bakeries,” the Greek said while pointing toward a few remaining Italian restaurants. "This is all that's left, a couple restaurants and one bakery. It's a fucking shame."

As the Greek reminisced, we continued to inch along Main Street.

"And this used to be safe, too. You could take your family here. People would come from miles around to go shopping or eat. Now look at it," he said as we passed a Spanish bodega with a homeless man walking along the sidewalk in front of it. The man was pushing a shopping cart full of junk, his only possessions.

"So, what happened?" I asked.

"The fucking liberals, they're what happened. Liberal politicians and liberal judges took over Massachusetts. Nowadays, if we make an arrest, they treat us like *we're* criminals. And the judges won't send anyone to jail."

"Got it."

"In the old days, when I started, thirty years ago, if someone stole a necklace, all I'd need to do is find him, tell him to turn himself in at the P.D., and by the end of the day he'd be there! He knew that if he didn't show up, there'd be hell to pay.

"How's that?"

Patrick Burns

"If he didn't show up at the front desk to meet the Sergeant by 4:00 PM, and you had to go find him and chase him down, he'd better be wearing a turban when you brought in front of the Desk Sergeant the next day."

The Greek chuckled at the image he offered.

"A turban?"

"Yeah, he'd better be wearing a bandage on his head when you brought him in, or *you'd* be on the carpet next!" The Greek laughed as our vehicle coasted into a dirt lot. "We'll hide behind the boarded-up gas station and wait for the signal to move in."

Time passed. The 10:30 scheduled meeting time came and went. As it did, Lewis pressed Carlos to get the target to show up. But so far, his phone calls went unanswered. Another hour passed. It was now lunchtime, and soon the streets would be filled with pedestrians and school kids.

Finally, the radio crackled with static briefly before transmitting a voice from one of the other team members.

"Rob! It's unit one," said the young Springfield officer riding a bicycle in circles under the Route 91 exit ramp.

"Go, Eddie," Lewis replied using his hand-held two-way radio, still crouched down in the rear of the van. As he waited for Eddie's reply, he stood and peeked out the rear window.

"He just passed by here," Eddie reported, gasping for breath as he peddled his bike on the sidewalk. "He'll be turning onto Main Street after the red light changes any second now. I'm right behind him."

But sooner than expected, the target turned a corner, avoiding the light.

"Anyone else have an eyeball?" Lewis asked everyone.

"Chappy!" Lewis shouted. "He's coming your way. Do you see him?"

"Not yet, Rob. There's a lot of traffic. I can only see a half a block from here."

"Anyone?" Lewis asked.

"It's Eddie," a voice on the radio said, trying to catch his breath while peddling faster. "I'm right behind him. He's approaching the Nunez bodega. We're a block away."

"Arrest team, Burns and Steve, start pulling out and heading toward the alley," Lewis ordered. "Don't pull into the alley until Chappy confirms the target is in the trap!"

As Eddie continued peddling closer, he saw the driver's face. He then checked for any other occupants. "Guys, it's him," he declared. "But it looks like there may be a baby in the back seat. I can see the top of a car seat."

Inside each unit, all the team members' faces dropped as they realized the mission possibly would be aborted. A baby in the car was not anticipated. It would be too dangerous.

"Chappy, you need to confirm if there is or isn't a baby in that seat before I give the go for the arrest team," Lewis instructed.

"Got it," Chapdelaine acknowledged as he scanned the vehicles in traffic heading his way on Main Street.

Lewis again pulled back the curtain to check the alley. There was no sign of the target. A large box truck was parked next to one of the delivery entrances to the stores.

"Hey," Lewis shouted. "Did anyone see where that yellow truck came from? Anyone see a driver?"

"I saw a large yellow truck pass my location a few minutes ago," Chappy responded.

An armed trafficker was moments away from the take-down location. He might have a baby in the back seat. And now, an unexpected delivery truck was parked in the middle of the scene, with the driver's location unknown.

"Nobody moves in!" Lewis ordered. "I repeat, nobody moves in! Hold your positions!"

"He's at the alley!" Chappy announced as he rushed to shift his car into gear while unsnapping the holster for his .40 caliber. "He's pulling into the alley!"

The teams snapped into action as they rushed to the alleyway. Eddie peddled his bike as fast as he could along the sidewalks and cut through several traffic gaps. The Greek and I were already on Main Street, just ten yards from the target's car. Slowly, we pulled in behind it.

"Not too close," the Greek advised as we closed in on the target's van. "Go slower!"

Only one person was visible. We could see the driver. But we had no view of the baby's car seat. *Was it empty? Was there a baby in it?* Time seemed to stand still as we slowly followed the target's van down the narrow alley toward the parking lot at the end. Lewis and the informant watched out the undercover van's window.

"I see the target approach. I see the car seat. It's empty. Everyone, green light!" said Lewis.

There was no going back. Whatever would happen would happen now!

Inside the yellow delivery truck blocking the second entrance, the driver, beyond anyone's view, was deep inside the cargo section, busy loading a stack of clean linens onto a cart. He had no idea what was about to happen.

As soon as we reached the rear of the alley, the target's brake lights came on. Greek and I leaped from our vehicle and sprinted toward his.

"Police! Police!" we yelled as we ran to the van with our guns drawn and pointed at the driver.

"That's it. We've got him now," I thought to myself as I felt relieved that it was over. He had no way to escape; the only two alleys for a possible escape were both blocked. The large, yellow box truck blocked the rear alley, and a DEA car was parked in the middle of the other.

But before we had time to close the 10-yard gap between the two vehicles, the driver grabbed the shift and revved the engine. I looked down and saw his red brake lights go out as the white back-up lights came on instead. *"Shit!"* I thought. *"He's trying to run us over!"*

The engine revved louder as he hit the gas pedal and sent his car speeding toward us. I turned on my heels and made a dash back toward our car, diving into the open door at the last second before his car sped by me, missing my feet by inches as it raced by.

Laying down across my passenger seat after diving in, I watched the target spin his car around. He paused a moment to look for an escape route. But the box truck was blocking the rear alley. So he headed back toward the alleyway leading to Main Street, the alley we had just come through, but the DEA blocker car was already in place.

Eddie had been in the alley as our back-up. The driver sped toward him. Eddie picked up his bicycle and threw it at the approaching van. The van smashed into it in midair, and then it continued forward and ran the bike over, mangling it on the pavement as Eddie dove for cover.

The car disappeared into the middle of the alley.

As I hopped back out of our car and followed it on foot, I knew the alley was blocked. I thought, *"Okay. Now, we've got him for sure."*

But before I reached his van, I heard the crash as the driver had plowed into the DEA blocker car midway down the alley.

His tires screeched. Smoke and the odor of burnt-rubber wafted into the air. He tried to use his van as a plow to push the DEA car the length of the alley to Main Street for his escape.

Patrick Burns

Metal clashed, wheels spun and smoked, but the van did little to move the other car. It didn't have enough power to proceed any further. *"OK. This has to be it!"* I thought.

Chappy ran to the driver's window and smashed it out with the butt of his pistol. He pointed it at the driver's head. The barrel was only inches from his head.

Eddie did the same on the passenger side front window.

With two guns pointing at his temples, fingers on the triggers, and voices yelling at him to put up his hands, I felt sure this was finally over. But to be sure, I ran up to the rear of his van, drew my weapon, and aimed at the back of his head.

I could see pedestrians and cars passing along on Main Street, ten yards away in my peripheral view. "Police! Don't Move! Driver! Put your hands up!" Chappy and Eddie yelled to the driver.

He raised his hands then suddenly grabbed hold of the gear shift. He pushed it upward into reverse. I glanced away from the sites of my gun and saw the backup lights come on. The engine roared.

"Shit!" I muttered.

The officers at the front windows couldn't react, and they couldn't fire without risking shooting each other. As they dove to the sides of the alley to avoid being squashed by the moving vehicle, I checked the sights on my gun. *I still might have a shot at his head.* I thought. But in my peripheral view, I can see pedestrians and children walking along the sidewalk. Cars were passing by on Main Street. If I missed, I would likely hit an innocent person.

This all happened in a fraction of a second—shoot or don't shoot. Shoot him, and I could be saving all of our lives. Miss him, and it will be a disaster.

As the van accelerated toward me, I turned and ran for my life.

Ten yards to the end of the alley—which may not seem like much, but with a racing minivan behind you trying to kill you—it seemed much longer.

Finally, I reached the end of the alley, jumping over Eddie's mangled bicycle on my way to diving behind a dumpster.

"You okay, Pat?" I hear a familiar voice as I hit the ground. I looked up, it was the Greek. He had his gun drawn, taking cover behind the same dumpster.

As the van backed into the open lot area, I could see the driver's face through his front window. The van now faced us. The driver's eyes were searching the surroundings, considering his next move.

Patrick Burns

A moment later, he put the gear into drive again and headed in my direction. I stepped out from behind the trash bin as Chappy left the alley. We took positions in front of the van.

It accelerated toward us.

"Bang! Bang, ba-bang, bang, bang!" shots rang out. Chappy let out a sound of excruciating pain as he folded over, grabs the side of his abdomen, and fell to the ground.

"I'm hit," he said while cringing in agony, curled up on the asphalt.

I aimed at the driver's head. This time I fired. But the van was moving too fast, and I missed. It continued circling the parking lot as other officers arrived on the scene. He was surrounded by guns now.

It became a shooting gallery as the driver tried to run us down with his car while bullets whizzed by from every direction. Some landed inside the yellow box truck's open cargo door and ricocheted off the wood walls. The rounds exploded as they hit the walls, sending chards of wood flying through the air like shrapnel. The delivery man, unknown to us, was inside the truck's cargo section loading hand towels onto a carrier. Hearing the bullets fly by his head, he dove to the floor.

Outside his truck, bullets continued to riddle the trafficker's van as he sped around the parking lot, looking for an escape. One bullet ripped into his steering column just inches from him. Another smashed through the windshield. Officer Chapdelaine lay helpless on the asphalt, grasping his side and cringing in pain as the van whirled around him and bullets flew overhead.

Finally, the trafficker headed for the six-foot stockade fence. I remained standing next to Chappy, in the right position for another clear shot at him through the van's rear window. I fired. The van approached the wooden fence. I fired again. It crashed through the wooden fence. I fired again.

The van plowed over the fence and ran over some children's toys on the other side. Finally, it was stopped by a chain-link fence just beyond.

Some of the team rushed to Officer Chapdelaine's side to slow the bleeding as the wailing sound of an ambulance could be heard approaching in the distance.

The van was riddled with bullets and disabled. The wounded trafficker lay motionless in the driver's seat, his head slumped against the side window. Moments later, the ambulance arrived, and the emergency squad rushed to Chappy's aid.

As the Greek and I remained standing in the carnage, he looked over at me for a moment,

Patrick Burns

“Welcome to Springfield, Pat!”

4   *Shots Fired*

That took care of the drug trafficking activities. But it was not the end of the investigation.; someone supplied him with illegal weapons. A new group of Russian mobsters had moved into the west side of town. They were prime suspects.

After the mêlée, the wounded and bandaged gangster was brought limping into state court. Later, at his trial, he was convicted of six counts of attempted murder of law enforcement officers.

One count was for trying to run me over with the van. He received 10 years in state prison.

It was time to search for new targets. Generally, the search began by looking through crime reports for leads to gun traffickers unless a tip came in from the public or another law enforcement agency, which was often the case.

I kept hoping for a lead on the Russian case, but nothing came in.

When a firearm is seized by the local police departments in the surrounding areas, they prepare and then submit a crime-gun report to the local ATF office. It includes all the needed details about the seizure circumstances, including the crime committed and a complete description of the weapon. With that information in hand, I'd start the ATF gun tracing process while looking for new cases/targets.

But first, all the information from the local reports needed to be sent to ATF's National Firearms Tracing Center via electronic submission. This process included typing the information into my laptop computer, including each gun's manufacturer name, its make, model, caliber, and unique serial number.

After an hour of sitting alone at my desk one morning, typing in the incoming gun seizure reports, I made the final keystroke. Moments later, the data went from my desk in Springfield, MA, to a remote location 400 miles away in Martinsburg, West Virginia. It was received inside a compound of warehouse-sized buildings, where an army of workers began the gun trace process.

The federal government doesn't maintain a national gun registry. It's prohibited by law. So a National Tracing Center (NTC) is needed to manually research the history of each gun seized in a crime.

Workers do it via phone calls. They start by calling the gun manufacturer. With imported weapons, they call the company that imported the gun. Every gun in America must have a stamp engraving the manufacturer or importer's name and location that put the gun into circulation. From that point, the importer or manufacturer searches their records to identify which retail gun shop this gun went to. The tracing officer then contacts the retail gun shop to find the last known purchaser. That completes the trace.

Analysis of tracing reports allows looking for patterns, similar names, and such. In looking at a stack of trace reports, I came across the name of a Springfield man who seemed to have been buying an unusual number of weapons. The information indicated all the purchases took place at a couple of the local gun shops on the west side of town.

Without further delay, I made my way to the basement parking garage, used my electronic key pass to raise the metal overhead security door, waved to the blue-jacketed security guard standing on the opposite side, and headed to the west side.

*****

As I searched for my next gun trafficker, a few miles away, Detective Sean Condon, also known as "Hutch" from the famed TV show, drove his banged-up, battle-worn, blue Crown Vic into the south side of town hunting for his next target.

As he rounded a corner, he cautiously entered the Hollywood section in the city's south end, an urban jungle of high-rises filled with drug dens and shooting galleries. The turf was ruled by the Latin Kings, so it was one of his favorite hunting spots. As he arrived, the duct-taped mirror dangling from the passenger side—a casualty of one of his more recent car chases—announced his presence by clanging against the door.

Many apartments were abandoned, used as drug distribution sites or as shooting galleries. Inside, heroin addicts could buy drugs and use safe rooms to shoot up. The dilapidated rooms—around the clock—were littered with used syringes and unconscious customers sleeping off the high.

Outside in the dirt lots, residents, dealers, addicts, and criminals mingle all day and night. As one of them heard Condon's cruiser pulling into the neighborhood, he called out, alerting the others as he runs toward an alley. "Salt and Pepper, Salt and Pepper!"

But today, Pepper wasn't there. He was on his way to the State Police Academy. So Condon continued alone, slowly rounding the corner into Hollywood, heading toward the looming perimeter of high-rise apartments. As he did, his eyes were alert for a target.

As his car rolled further into the enemy territory, a man shouted a warning; vagrants and hoodlums scattered to the dark alleys. Others, seated on exposed decrepit wooden staircases and balconies, simply enjoyed watching the show. Some sipped Colt 45 while smoking dope, sitting on broken, ripped living room furniture on the outdoor porches.

"This is unit 521," Condon announced over his car radio to the dispatcher. "I'm in the Hollywood block."

"Roger unit 521," she replied.

As Condon rounded the last corner in the block, his presence became known to the next group standing along the roadside. Like the others, most began briskly walking away in different directions. But one teenager seemed oblivious to his presence. Condon spotted him immediately. He was standing next to his bicycle, deeply engaged in playing a video game on his cell phone. As the others scattered, Condon's instinct locked onto the straggler. Like a lion closing in on a young, unsuspecting antelope, he eased his Crown Vic toward the kid.

Condon noticed the kid's appearance from a distance. He was young, probably unemployed. He was in a high crime drug area and wearing a pair of sparkling expensive Nike sneakers. They seem to be worth at least as much as the abandoned cars parked nearby. While his prey remained unaware, alone, and exposed, Condon quietly moved in closer. Then, without a word, he opened his car door, casually stepped out of his cruiser, and approached the suspect on foot.

By the time the kid realized what was happening, it was too late. Suddenly, noticing the approaching footsteps, his head jerked upward. His eyes widened with shock, and he immediately turned his bike in the opposite direction, preparing to flee. But it was too late, as Condon reached up and grabbed hold of the handlebar.

"Whoa, buddy, hold on," Condon orders. "You live here?"

"Me?"

"Yeah, you. Who else is here? What's your name and address?"

As Condon kept the questioning going, he patted the youngster down for weapons.

"Oh, so, what's this?" Condon asks as he holds up a bag of weed from the kid's pants pocket.

"Ah, that's for personal use," the boy nervously replied.

Just then, the radio dispatcher's voice could be heard making a call-out, seeking any unit to respond to a nearby armed robbery in progress. Condon knew the location. It was just around the corner.

"Dispatch," Condon replies in his hand-held radio, "this is 521. I'll take it. I'm a block away!"

"Listen, kid, I'm gonna take this weed."

He reached into his pocket and retrieves a business card. "This is my number. I'm gonna keep this weed in evidence for one year. If you bring me some good information before the year is up, we can forget about this. If you don't, I'll be back to arrest you."

Condon jogged to his car, hopped into the driver's seat, and sped away, disappearing around the corner as he headed toward the armed robbery in progress.

*****

Relieved at his lucky break, the kid hopped on his bike and headed toward a nearby neighborhood to get more product to sell.

Within minutes, he parked his bicycle against the stairway leading to the open porch and knocked on the door. A heavily tattooed Hispanic man known as El Loco appeared and invited him inside. El Loco had a single letter tattoo on each finger. A gold chain hung from his neck. Behind him, inside the living room, two young women sat on a broken couch. Each woman was holding a crying baby in her arms as the kid stepped into the smoke-filled room.

He glanced around at the clutter. Empty bottles, overflowing ashtrays, and piles of clothing lay on the floor. Several open Styrofoam take-out food containers were filled with chicken bones. A pile of dirty diapers was stacked in the kitchen sink. A.45 caliber pistol was on the table. The dealer had another gun tucked into his baggy pants, pulling them down far enough to show the color of his boxer shorts and his rounded ass above the belt loops.

"You sell all of it already?" he asked.

"Yep. Here's your money, and I need another bag," the kid replied while handing over a wad of cash removed from his sock that the cop missed.

The dealer put the cash into his pocket and removed a bag of dope from his other baggy pocket. He handed it to the kid without a word and then pointed toward the door, gesturing for the boy to leave.

"Yo, any of these guns for sale?" the kid asked.

"No. Thems if any blue shirts come at me. Theyz loaded with cop-killer bullets...go clean through a cop's bulletproof vest. I's gonna kill me some blue shirts."

Without another word, the kid left the house, got back on his bike, and peddled toward his drug sales corner in Hollywood.

On the other side of town, I was driving across the Memorial Bridge on my way to the west side. The sun glimmered off the ripples on the chocolate brown river below me as it wound through the city. Where it churned by the sewage treatment plant, a lighter colored foam bounced along the river's edge.

While the south end is run by Hispanic gangs such as Latin Kings, La Familia, and others, the west side is strictly Russian territory. At the end of a small strip mall on one corner of Main Street, I spotted my destination, AAA Guns.

I parked in the lot behind it that was also shared by the strip mall stores, including the adjacent business, the Russian Book and Video Store. Across the street was the Russian Bakery. All the Russian stores were a grim reminder of the open case.

A loud cowbell instantly rang above my head as I entered the gun store. Looking up, I saw big Dave Stewart behind one of the glass showcases. He's a giant, literally the size of a bear. His petite, white-haired wife was seated behind him at a small folding table. As always, she's busy updating the sales journals.

Walking through the store, I was surrounded by thousands of guns and hundreds of thousands of rounds of ammunition. The walls and glass showcases were all filled with every make, model, and caliber you could imagine.

As I neared the back of the store. Dave extended his large hand, the size of a catcher's mitt. As we shook hands, mine disappeared into his, as if I had a child's sized hand.

"What can I do for you, Pat?" he asked as I pulled away from his grip before he crushed my hand.

"I've got a couple of gun records here. Did anyone from the tracing center call you on this guy?" I handed Dave a report reflecting a customer named Raphael Perez.

Dave looks briefly at the report and then immediately hands it to his wife.

"Honey, pull up all the guns this customer purchased."

"Yes, Pat. I know him. But he hasn't been here in a month or so. My wife can give you a printout of everything he bought.

"What do you know about him?"

"Well, he works for one of the local armored truck companies. He came in a few times wearing his uniform. But I haven't seen him lately."

"Here you go, dear." His wife hands him a printout listing a couple of dozen guns of all makes and models.

"There must be thousands of dollars' worth of guns here, Dave. That's a lot of money for a security guard salary, don't you think?"

Dave nodded and put his finger to one side of his nose while looking me in the eye to see if his clue is registering.

"You think he uses drugs?"

He said nothing, just shrugged his shoulders as if to say, "You figure it out."

"Let me ask you a question. Did he ever come in with anyone else?" I know that if he's a gun trafficker, they often come in with their clients to allow them to view the guns beforehand.

"Always, Pat. He sometimes came in with his son. But he always came in with other people. They would look at the guns together before he'd make the purchase."

"Great. Thanks, Dave! Call me if he comes back!"

*****

As Detective Condon sat in on a briefing at the FBI office for an upcoming undercover drug deal, his cell phone rang.

"Officer Condon...It's me...Right, the guy on the bike..... I think I have what you want..." There was a short pause, then the caller continued. "What if I told you I know where you can find a cop killer? Would that get me off the hook?"

To cops, those words hit like a bolt of lightning.

"Stay right there," Condon says, "I'm on the way." Then he rushed out of the door.

Patrick Burns

Back at the ATF office, I continued researching the databases and reviewing the gun records for Raphael Perez. On each ATF purchase record, which he'd signed under oath, he'd claimed that the guns are all for his use, that he's employed as an armed guard, and that his firearm permit is therefore still valid.

As I summarized all of his purchases, I listed each gun's price, make, caliber, and model. The value alone seemed suspicious enough for a minimum wage earner.

After reviewing the records from the gun shop, I next searched through the local police report files. Sure enough, there were more red flags. Several hospital emergency rooms had filed complaints on Perez. He'd been shopping around, visiting multiple hospitals, claiming to be in pain, seeking Oxycodone.

So far, everything looked promising. I next called the armored car company where he claimed to be employed. After introducing myself and explaining the purpose of the call, the company owner replied.

"I'm sorry. I'd like to help you, but Mr. Perez no longer works for us. He hasn't worked here for over six months. Ralph was fired for threatening the other employees with his weapon. We had to let him go."

"Thank you very much."

Perez is unemployed, desperately seeking drugs while spending thousands of dollars on guns, and he's always accompanied by others at the gun shop. Bingo!

I called Dave at AAA Guns. "Dave, make sure you call me if you hear from him!"

"Will do, Pat. But like I told you, he hasn't been here in a few months. Did you try checking with Mike, down the road at Guns & Gun Parts?"

"Not yet. But I'm on my way. And thanks!"

*****

Back at the drug supplier's house, El Loco paced back and forth in the living room. The two women continued watching television, and their babies continued crying amid the smoke and garbage.

Occasionally, the dealer looked out the front window to check the street. Looking across his front porch to the road, he saw it was clear – no sign of customers or trouble. The neighbor directly across the street was casually washing his car. Everything seemed quiet.

The gangster let the curtain close, stepped back from the window, and took a large swig of his liter-sized Colt 45. He returned to pacing back and forth through the small apartment. But then a thunderous sound came through the front window. He rushed toward it with his gun drawn.

Patrick Burns

It was a caravan of a dozen or more dark-colored SUVs barreling down the street. Mixed in with them were a couple of state police cars and several local police cruisers. As the convoy roared up the road, the neighbor across the street dove into the back seat of his soapy car.

Tires screeched and doors could be heard opening as the vehicles drove right up on the lawn facing the dealer's front porch. Troopers and officers rushed the house and took up positions of cover surrounding the front porch. Condon and another officer ran along the house's side, heading toward the back yard to cover the rear doors, the likely route of escape.

As Condon rounded the home's rear corner, he remembered his body armor, resting on the front seat of his car. In a rush, he forgot to put it on. But now it was too late to go back for it. And it may not have mattered, anyway. This wanna-be cop-killer is said to have armor-piercing bullets.

Inside the house, El Loco checked his weapons. The women ran for cover as a wall of heavily armed officers and state troopers set up their perimeter. Knowing this gangster has said he will kill cops, every available officer responded.

Then El Loco headed to the rear door to escape, but, unknown to him, Condon was waiting there for him.

Now standing behind the house and facing the rear door, Condon and another officer could hear movement inside the apartment.

Condon approached the rear door, and as he raised his foot to kick it in, the door swung open in front of him. "Shit!"

Standing just inches apart, Condon and the cop killer were now face-to-face, both frozen for a moment and stunned from this unexpected turn of events.

Condon had never seen this man before, not even a picture of him. He's been given a general description; he's not even sure it's the right man. *He seems to match the description,* Condon thought to himself for a split-second.

Instinctively, he inspected the man's hands. And there it was, a .45 Caliber pistol. With lightning speed, since his life depended on it, Condon reached for his service weapon. As he did, the gangster slammed the door shut.

"Was that him?" Condon asked Jim Mazza, a muscular, running-back-sized officer standing nearby.

"I think so," replied Mazza.

Condon turned his attention back to the door; it was locked. He looked to the other officer and nodded, indicating he was going in. While holding his weapon in one hand, he raised his foot and kicked the door. The door didn't budge an inch. It was like kicking a cement wall, evidently bolted and locked. He kicked it again, nothing. He tried again, still nothing.

"You want me to try?" Mazza asked.

Condon gritted his teeth, holstered his pistol, and took a running jump toward the door.

"Boom!" it burst wide open.

But as it did, to both men's unfortunate surprise, the killer was still standing just on the other side. But now he had his.45 caliber pistol already raised to head-level and was pointing straight at Condon's face.

Condon froze for an instant. "Shit!"

He'd just finished holstering his service weapon to give himself more momentum as he charged the door. He was empty-handed, facing the barrel of a.45 just inches from his face. As he rushed to draw his gun out again, the suspect squeezed the trigger.

"Bang!"

Condon dove to his left, the bullet nearly grazing his head. He spotted a refrigerator near the door and leaped behind it while returning fire. The suspect fired again. Condon returned fire again, now from cover. As he did, he yelled the standard commands, "Drop your weapon! Get down on the floor!"

"We ARE on the floor! We're already on the floor!" Condon heard women's screams coming from the front room.

"What the hell?" Condon wondered. That kid on the bike never mentioned there were women and babies in the house. He had been firing right through the wall and might have hit one!

Shots continued as the women crouched lower on the floor while clutching their babies.

The suspect was now standing in the middle of the living room. Condon remained behind the cover offered by the refrigerator, bullets flying by his head. The women continued screaming. The babies continued crying. Outside the house, the officers in the front yard began an entry attempt through the front door. A few started cautiously walking down a narrow hall leading from the front porch to a front door. As they did, El Loco saw them through the window as they approached and he fired through the front door.

Officers fell back as bullets tore through the door while spraying them with wooden shrapnel.

As the front yard team returned to their positions, the suspect watched the window for their next move. Condon, seeing El Loco distracted, seized the opportunity. He made a run for it toward the front room to tackle the gunman.

Patrick Burns

Halfway to the living room, he slipped on a diaper and some chicken bones, "Fuck!"

After regaining his footing, he continued forward. But looking up, he saw that the gangster had heard his footsteps and turned his attention back toward him.

"Bang!" The cop-killer fired.

Again. Condon dove out of the way and narrowly evaded the bullets as he retreated back to the refrigerator. Crouched down behind it, he took a moment to inspect the wall next to him. A trail of bullet holes led right to his position. He was mere inches away from each bullet as he ran.

With Condon momentarily pinned down again behind the appliance, the suspect turned his attention back toward the front door. He'd driven the officers away from it with his gunfire, but he hadn't yet accomplished his goal to kill a "Blue Shirt."

So he opened the front door, walking out onto the front porch. As he stepped out, he saw the back of one straggler, the last officer who hadn't yet made it back to cover.

"Bang!" The suspect fired, hitting the officer. The wounded man screamed in pain as he clutched his leg to cover the blood squirting out, falling behind a tree.

The killer continued toward the front porch, firing as he did. Officers were taking cover. He fired again and made it to the center of the open porch.

One officer called out over the radio for an ambulance to assist the downed officer as the gunfight continued.

"Officer down, officer down! Shots fired. We need an ambulance!"

Sitting a few miles away at the ATF office, I heard the mêlée over the radio and rushed to the scene to assist. As the fight continued, the criminal got hit again and again. Finally, he tumbled off the porch.

As the gunfire fell silent and the chaos ended, the neighbors begin slowly coming out of their homes. The man in the car cautiously emerged from the back seat.

I arrived just as the ambulance rolled up. The EMTs jump out and rush to aid the shot officer. But they seem to be in no apparent rush to tend to their second client. He was patiently waiting atop the bush, riddled with thirty-two bullet holes.

5   *Honey, Your Package is Here*

Resting atop a small crest on the road, I spotted the short strip mall I'm looking for. *Guns & Gun Parts* is set on the corner, adjacent to a local bar. The sign over the bar's entrance reads "Collins Tavern." The significance of the name didn't strike me at the moment. But it would come in a little bit.

An elementary school was across the street; not an ideal place to be looking for bad guys and guns.

If Perez was shopping around for guns, AAA Guns and Guns & Gun Parts were the only gun stores in the area. Based on that fact alone, I decided to ask the owner if he's sold any guns to Perez.

As I parked my car in the side lot, I noticed a sign in the window of Collins Tavern. "Today's lunch special-ham sandwich with chips and pickle $1.50". I decided to have one.

A few minutes later, as I sit alone at the bar waiting for my sandwich, I read the captions on the black and white historical pictures all over the walls.

The first picture is of England's Prime Minister, Margaret Thatcher. Then I read the caption below it. *Wanted, Dead or Alive for Treason.*

What the hell?

I look to the next framed image. It's a picture of an old city, perhaps in Ireland. The caption reads, *"Not here, not in a taxi, not in your home, never speak of the cause because someone is listening..."*

Damn! I think to myself as I realized what kind of bar I was in.

Looking around at the surrounding walls, I saw they all had similar themes; newspaper clippings of various bombings and the carnage in Ireland's streets. Memorials to the struggle for Irish independence from British rule.

Michael Collins was an Irish revolutionary soldier, a leading figure in the early Irish struggle for independence. I got a sinking feeling in my gut; I was not in friendly territory. An ATF agent sitting alone in an Irish Republican Army (IRA) supporting bar is a bad idea.

I glanced toward the front door; a group stood in front of it. I eyed the back door.

Shit! I'm being watched. They're sending me a message; they know who I am, and they control this place.

Another small group of gray-haired, crusty old men talked among themselves. One of them intermittently gave me a cold stare. Clearly, they're talking about me. I wanted to get the hell out of there, but I didn't want to look like I was fleeing.

Just then, the bartender arrived with my ham sandwich, pickle, and chips. He gave me a hard look, dropping the plate onto the bar in front of me.

As I took a bite of the pickle—watching out of the corner of my eye—a tall man from the group approached me.

"What are you doing here?" he asked, his eyes narrow and a stern look on his face. The others in his group remained at the end of the bar, watching with cold stares and waiting to see what would happen.

Shit! I now recognize him.

And he knew exactly who I am. He was a retired Massachusetts State Trooper, a security guard at the federal courthouse – one of the "blue jackets," the guys dressed in gray slacks and a blue sports jacket. I had seen him at his post at the metal detectors at the front entrance.

Each morning he saw me arrive and go around the x-ray machines because I'm armed. He recognized me as soon as I came into the bar. And as soon as he did, he alerted the others.

The Boston area was full of Irishmen, and there were many supporters for freeing Northern Ireland.

Some of the IRA sympathizers included people from law enforcement. Evidently, this was one of them.

"Just having lunch. Nothing more."

He gives me a skeptical look, turned his back on me, and returned to his group.

In short order, I finished lunch, threw five dollars on the bar, and get the hell out of there. Fortunately, it was only a few steps to a friendlier location. *Guns & Gun Parts* was just next door, and I'd met the owner many times.

When I entered the tiny, dingy room, Mike was seated just a few feet away, reading the classified ads.

"Hi, Mike, how's business?" I asked, squeezing between racks of gun accessories as I made my way to the back of the store.

His entire shop was about the size of a one-car garage. He was always dressed frugally; thick glasses, a wrinkled shirt, and sporting a disheveled comb-over hairstyle. The rickety wooden shop floor looks like it hasn't seen a broom in a month. Inside the showcase was just a few old guns that looked like something you'd find abandoned in an alley.

"Hiya Pat. I'm good, ah, ya know," he replied in his unusual accent, sounding more like a Minnesotan than someone from Massachusetts. "What'd you need?"

Patrick Burns

Mike keeps his expensive, high-quality guns under the counter out of view from his seedy clientele. He took a moment to show me a new 9 mm Ruger, a Tec 9 auto pistol, and a.50 caliber Desert Eagle. The barrel on the Desert Eagle is large enough to fit an index finger inside of it. It's a hand-cannon firing a.50 caliber slug that will easily pass through a car door then go clean through both sides of a policeman's body armor.

"I'm wondering if you've seen a particular guy in here recently. His name is Raphael Perez."

"Well Pat, ah, ya know, sure, sure. He's been here. He was here a few days ago."

"Was he alone?"

"Actually, he was with his son."

"That's it?"

"Come to think of it, he was also with another guy. He ordered this 9mm Ruger."

"He bought it?"

"Yeah. Well, he paid for it, but I told him I needed three days to get the results back from the FBI background check. After that, he could come to pick it up."

"So he's coming back to pick it up?" I asked while trying not to reveal how important this was to me.

"Ya, sure, called this morning. I told him the background check was all good. He said he'd be coming back after lunch today to pick it up."

"Great! Make me a copy of that ATF form. I'll be in the area. Call me as soon as he comes back in to pick up the gun," I said as I rushed out the door.

The last thing I wanted to do is bump into Perez now before he picked up the gun.

I checked my watch. Perez could arrive at any moment. There was no time to spare. There was not enough time to get any help from ATF. I was working alone in the Springfield office. The closest other office was 50 miles away in Worchester.

Besides that problem, I had another more pressing situation. After ATF's botched arrest of the Branch Davidians in Waco, Texas, where scores of men, women, and children were killed, ATF cracked down on enforcement operations to ensure more oversight. Any arrest or enforcement operation now required advance approval from Division Headquarters. My division was in Boston.

But there was no time to ask for approval. That would usually take several days. This gun that Perez was about to pick up would be long gone by then. It would likely be on the street and in the hands of a criminal. Someone could be killed with it before I got the needed approval from Boston.

My choice was clear. I either let this guy go while I apply for approval or handle it on my own without it. Concealing it from Boston also meant I couldn't reveal my operation by asking for backup. I'd need to do this alone. There was no other way.

I scanned the area for a suitable spot to set up my surveillance. Collins Tavern would have been perfect. But that was a no-go. The school across the street seemed to be a good location. But if the students filled the parking lot, it would be a problem. Parking in Mike's lot would be too close. I'd be seen.

Looking down the hill, I spotted a gas station and convenience store with a clear line of sight. I could sip coffee like the other customers and just sit in my car watching the front door of Guns & Gun Parts, waiting for Perez.

The only downside to selecting this gas station was that it was on the opposite side of the road from the gun shop. If the suspect left the gun store and headed down the hill instead of heading further up the hill, I'd be on the wrong side of the road. I'd need to cross a lane of heavy traffic, which might cause a long delay, and risk losing him in traffic.

It was a 50/50 shot as to which direction he'd go. But one way or another, I needed to witness him getting the gun. Then, hopefully, I could see a transfer to another person. The gas station was where I'd set up to start the attempt.

An hour later, after seeing no signs of Perez, I called the shop.

"Mike, it's Pat. Any updates?" I asked as I sipped on my Big Gulp coffee while still parked across the road.

"Well, not yet."

More time passed. Finally, a red Camaro pulled up to the curb in front of the gun shop. I raised my camera to take a picture.

I watched the driver get out, and snapped another picture. A moment later, the driver, who I can only assume is Perez, reached into the car's back seat. A little boy, presumably his son, took his hand and got out. I took another photo.

As Perez and his son walked to the entrance, another man stepped out of the car's passenger side. His arms were covered with tattoos. He was dressed in red and white colored shorts and shirt, colors I recognized as associated with one of the local gangs, "La Familia," "the family." I took another picture.

Time passed with no call from Mike. The car was still parked out front. More time passed. Finally, I called.

"Hi, Mike, it's me. Is that the guy? Is he getting the gun or not?"

"Hi, honey. Yes, your package is here."

"Is he buying the gun?"

"Yes."

"Great. Let me know when they're about to leave."

"Sure, honey. I'll bring some milk home with me when I come."

The suspect, I realized, must have been standing inches away from Mike.

Fifteen minutes later, I snapped a photo as the door to the gun shop opened. Out came the driver, identified by Mike as Raphael Perez. Right behind him was the boy and the unidentified tattooed Hispanic man.

I took a picture of Perez carrying a shopping bag, then I called Mike.

"Does he have the gun?

"Yes, Pat. It's in the bag."

Perez started the car and pulled away from the curb. Hoping he would turn around and go up the hill, I waited. If he heads my way, I could fall in behind him in traffic.

I edged up to the parking lot exit, watching the red Camaro. He headed down the hill, in the opposite lane from where I was, and I would need to cross traffic before I can follow him. This is precisely what I had hoped would not happen.

Although I knew the gun was in the car, I still had no crime. Perez had a permit and could possess firearms. He had committed no crime until he handed the gun over to the gangster. Somehow, I needed to witness the transfer.

I nudged through the traffic and into the southbound lane, a few cars behind the red Camaro. *So far, so good.* Both of us were inching along in bumper-to-bumper traffic. Up ahead, the traffic light turned red. When it turned green, we approached a four-way intersection. On the left side was a gas station. I knew he wasn't going right because he could have turned right on the red. I was hoping he would go straight.

Our two cars inched along. Just when I thought I was in luck, Perez pulled into the gas station. I was now at the intersection with a green light, and I needed to keep going while not losing sight of the car. This surveillance was only beginning, yet it was falling apart already.

The boy and passenger remained in the car as Perez filled the tank. Back at the traffic light, now headed in the opposite direction, I got his license plate info and jotted it down.

"This is Burns," I said, calling the Worchester office. "Can someone run a license plate for me?"

Perez finished pumping gas and got back in the car; I was stuck at the light. He took a left down a side street and disappeared; I fought my way through the traffic and tried to catch up, but the Camaro was gone.

"ATF unit, we have the information you requested," the radio dispatcher announced.

"Go ahead."

"We have the address for the vehicle registration you requested."

I searched every side street, to no avail. In fifteen minutes, I found myself in a typical residential city neighborhood looking for the right house. I rolled slowly through while reading the house numbers. Once I found it, there was no car in the driveway and no sign of the red Camaro.

I continued to the end of the short road and pulled around the corner. I was far enough from the house to not be spotted but close enough to have a view. I took a photo of the house in case I need a description for a search warrant. Then, I waited.

It was quiet; no traffic passing by and no pedestrians walking the street. I hoped no one would notice an unfamiliar car parked on their corner. This was the only place that would give me a chance to pick up his trail again and see if he still had the gun.

Suddenly, I heard a car approaching, coming from the far end of the street.

Please be a red Camaro!

As it came into view, my prayer was answered. I eased down in my seat and picked up the camera. A few seconds later, the suspect's car stopped directly in front of the red, single-family house. I took another picture. A moment later, the driver's door swung open, and Perez stepped out. I took another picture. He paused a moment, looked around, and then reached inside the car. Out came his small son, holding his father's hand. I took another photo.

Next, I focused the lens on the passenger seat. It was empty. Perez and his son walked to the house, but the other man was gone along with the shopping bag with the gun. I balanced my camera on the steering wheel and snapped a final photo.

6   *He's Got Twenty-Four Hours*

Raphael Perez was a gun trafficker, an unemployed drug addict trading guns to drug dealers for drugs. The firearms he put onto the street were in dangerous criminals' hands and posed an imminent threat to the public.

But I couldn't confront him at this point because I could prove nothing. Contacting him then would have only diminished, if not killed, any chance for an arrest or the recovery of the weapons.

Perez had no legal obligation to speak to me. He likely would not cooperate, and I didn't have enough to use to pressure him to do so, not yet. The only thing I could prove was that he bought a lot of guns with his valid permit.

The next step had to be a return visit to Guns & Gun Parts.

"Hi, Mike, thanks for your help. But I need you to describe the man you saw with Perez when he bought the 9mm?"

"Well, he was average."

"Average? How about his age, build?"

"I'd say kinda thin, maybe in his 20's."

"Okay. He's average. How about any distinguishing marks, scars, tattoos?"

"Come to think of it, he did have tattoos. They were on his arms?"

"Do you remember what the tattoos looked like?"

"One of them said something like 'Freaky.' I don't know what the other arm said. But I remember it because I was wondering what 'Freaky' meant."

"Thanks! That's it for now. Let me know if you see or hear from Perez again."

"Pat," Mike said, as I turned to rush out the door.

"What's that?"

"Perez ordered more guns. He's coming back for a Tec 9 and a Desert Eagle.50 caliber."

"He's coming back? When?"

"I told him it takes a few days to get the clearance from the FBI. Said I'd call him when they were ready."

Perfect!

This time I'd have a few days before his return, enough time to get the approval for surveillance.

"Thanks again, Mike."

I headed out the door to return to the Springfield courthouse to get busy preparing the request. The request is called an Operational Plan, aka "OP Plan." They are rarely completed and approved in such a short time frame. They're incredibly detailed and very time-consuming.

Op Plans need to include everything right down to closest hospitals and blood types of all the suspects and agents involved, maps of the city, and much more.

After preparation, they need to be approved at several levels. The process often takes weeks. But a three-day window was all that we had. We needed to have it done and approved before Perez came for his guns.

So the clock was ticking. As I waited for Boston's approval, I continued looking through the database to identify the second suspect. I used the only thing I had to go on, searching for any gang member in the system with a "Freaky" tattoo on his arm.

Eventually, the screen displayed an image of the right forearm of a La Familia Gang member. It belonged to Frank Jimenez, a.k.a. Freaky Ti.

Bingo!

I continued reading the report. It also indicated that the "Ti" part of Freaky Ti's street name was an abbreviation for "Thai Stick." Other information revealed that Freaky was a fugitive from justice. He had an outstanding warrant for state drug and weapons charges.

Freaky didn't know it yet, but he was about to add federal gun charges to his resume. That is, of course, if I could find him. There was no current address in the database, nothing in the records to reveal his current whereabouts.

There was nothing -- he was a fugitive, on the run. I didn't know where he was, but I did know he was in hiding, desperate, and armed and dangerous.

*****

As I waited for the approval call from Division Headquarters, a few miles away, in the city of Holyoke, MA, a young kid lingered inside a covered doorway in a rough section of town. He worked the same corner each day, peddling heroin.

Puffing on a fat blunt and sipping on a one-liter bottle of Colt.45, the youngster watched the traffic pass by as he waited for the next customer. Behind him, his La Familia gang graffiti logo was freshly painted over an older Latin King gang logo. The corner has been recently claimed by his gang.

As he worked from the doorway for much of the day, making sales, earning money, and not expecting trouble, all seemed good. But later in the day, a problem arose. When he heard another car approaching, he first thought it was just another customer. But this time, the occupants weren't coming to buy heroin.

As the car rolled up, the driver, James Ortiz, and his brother, Jason, smiled and waved to the kid. The boy smiled and waved back, still believing they were customers. The car continued and then pulled up to the curb to stop near him.

Jason, seated on the passenger side with the window open, smiled again and leaned out of his open window while flashing a hand gesture. He shaped his index finger and thumb of one hand into the shape of an L. He used his other hand to make a shape that vaguely resembled an F, the initials for La Familia.

Delighted to see he was among fellow gang members, the kid smiled even more broadly and returned the hand signal.

Immediately, Jason dropped the smile. His suspicions confirmed—this guy was a La Familia poacher—Jason's hands disappeared below the open window.

A moment later, they reappeared, holding a loaded 9mm pistol and pointing it at the boy.

The boy saw the gun and tried to run. The Latin King fired, hitting him in the leg. He remained standing, clutching his leg while screaming in pain. Jason fired again. The second shot hit him in the shoulder. The boy remained standing still, now crying and grasping at his shoulder in pain. Ortiz emptied the remaining rounds into his victim.

With the kid now lifeless and silent on the sidewalk, the passenger car door swung open, and Ortiz casually stepped out, carrying a spray paint can in one hand and the 9mm in his other.

After stepping callously over the boy, he walked directly to the doorway. Ortiz shook the can a couple of times and then painted the Latin King logo on the wall above the boy's body.

A moment later, the two brothers drove off.

"This is Latin King turf, motherfucker!" James yelled as he hit the gas pedal and pulled the car from the curb.

"Did you see how many times I had to shoot him?" Jason said as he tucked the gun under his seat. "Bitch wouldn't go down!"

"We need a bigger gun, bro."

"Damn straight!"

"I know what we need. It's called a Desert Eagle, yo. It's a.50 cal, blow a hole clear through a brick wall," Jason says.

"Where we get dat?"

"I know a guy. The dude's a cop or security guard or something. He's my customer. Just need to give the dude some powder. Das it." Jason said as they continue cruising the streets, looking for any other poachers on Latin King turf.

*****

It's 9:00 AM, three days since Raphael Perez purchased the gun with Freaky. Our team of agents and officers were all in place. Each two-man unit was in an unmarked car, parked in the perimeter surrounding Guns & Gun Parts, ready to follow the target in every possible direction.

I was back at the convenience store/gas station across the street, watching the building's front and the shop's entrance. I saw Mike arrive and park in the adjacent lot. Moments later, I watched as he put his key into the store's front door.

"All units, we are open for business," I relayed over the radio as Mike disappeared inside the store.

"Copy, Pat, we're ready," replied the salty detective from Springfield P.D., Steve M., a.k.a. The Greek. He's parked on a side street a block away. Steve is teamed up with a former Boston P.D. officer, ATF Special Agent, Jack Moran.

Other units chimed in, acknowledging the message.

Hours passed with no activity. Sipping coffee and eating bag lunches, we all held in place. Just after lunchtime, a red Camaro rolled up to the curb in front of the gun store.

"Our guy has arrived. Stand by," I announced, snapping a few pictures of Raphael Perez.

As the passenger door opened next, I snapped a picture of a young Hispanic male dressed in gold and black colored clothes.

"Looks like we have Perez arriving," I told the team. "But he's with a Latin King. It's not Freaky today."

A moment later, the two men approached the front door. I took more pictures as evidence. They disappeared inside.

As they entered, Mike was seated on the other side of the room behind the glass display case. The phone chimed.

"Yellooow! Guns and Gun Parts!" Mike answered as Perez and his customer approached him, standing a few inches away, just on the other side of the display case.

"Mike, it's me, Pat. Is that Perez? Is he going to pick up the guns today?"

"Hi, honey. Yes. Your package is here now. I'll bring it home later."

"Are they getting both guns?"

"Yes, honey. I'll see you at home later. I have customers right now. I can't talk."

"So he's getting the .50 caliber Desert Eagle and the Tec 9?"

"Yes, honey. Yes. ...chicken is fine... I love you too," Mike hung up the phone and waited on his customers who had been watching him the whole time.

"All units, they're getting both guns. Stand by. I'll advise when they leave the store."

"Copy, Pat," the Greek replied.

We knew that with so many units surrounding the area, following the suspects after they left the store should have been easy. But we also knew these things never go as they should.

It would be convenient if we could just grab them as they left the store. But that would be a fatal mistake. No crime will have been committed because Perez would still have possession of the guns.

Patrick Burns

That meant we'd need to wait for the transfer. And somehow, we'd need to witness it. Only then could we swoop in, make the arrest, and seize the weapons.

But witnessing the transfer could prove to be impossible. They could easily do it beyond our view. They could walk into a house or apartment. They could do it on the street inside the car, below the window level, where we wouldn't be able to see the bag or contents.

One thing was sure. Those guns could not fall into the hands of a criminal right under the noses of a dozen ATF agents. We would grab these guys at some point. But it had to be the right moment.

"The door is opening," I alerted the team. "Stand by."

"Copy. Copy. Copy," each unit acknowledged.

"Perez is carrying a shopping bag," I continued to relay the information over the radio.

I redialed the store phone.

"Mike, does he have the guns?"

"He's got them."

"Thanks!"

"All units, they have the guns, a .50 caliber and a Tec 9," I advised the team. "The guns are in the yellow shopping bag. Repeat, the guns are in the bag."

"Copy Pat. This is the Greek. We're right behind him, headed east on 20."

"We see the Camaro," another unit just east of the Greek said. "We'll fall in behind Steve."

For the second time, the red Camaro headed down Route 20 for a short distance. It then turned left into a residential neighborhood. The caravan of units followed loosely, balancing the risk of being spotted with the risk of losing contact.

Each time a turn was made by the Camaro, the following car continued straight to allow another team to move up and take over the eyeball. For fifteen minutes, the slow caravan of units leapfrogged through the back streets of Springfield. All was going smoothly, but then...

"He's gone!" one unit announced. "We've lost him at the red light at Route 5!"

The teams scrambled to spot the red Camaro. No one could find it. Finally, another unit said over the radio, "We've got him! He's getting on the highway, 390 North toward Holyoke!"

Minutes later, the red car and ATF units left the highway. I took over the eyeball, knowing that whatever has transpired inside that red car was beyond anyone's view.

We may have missed our opportunity.

As the Camaro neared a more residential neighborhood, I was right behind it.

Patrick Burns

"He's turning left on Maple Street." I alerted everyone. "It's a one-way, and he's going the wrong way on it!"

If I followed him down the wrong way on a one-way neighborhood street, he would notice me, so I parked at the corner, far away, but still close enough to see the car. A moment later, it pulled to the curb. The passenger door swung open. The man with gold and black gang colors stepped out.

"He's getting out. He's got the yellow bag!"

"We see him. We'll grab him!" The Greek was certain.

"I'll stay with the red car!" I announced as I saw Perez's red car pulling away from the curb. I hit the gas. Our covert operation was now over. Now it was game on, a full-speed chase.

Perez looked up in his rearview mirror, and I saw him looking right at me, wide-eyed. With the covert phase of this operation now over, I put the gas pedal to the floor and sped down the wrong way on the one-way street.

Perez saw me barreling down in his direction, and he also hit the gas. His tires screeched as he sped away. Seconds later, his car reached the corner, and I saw the brake lights come on. With skidding tires and smoking rubber, the car slid around the corner out of my view.

Three seconds later, my car reached the same corner. I glanced in the direction he headed, but he was gone. I had lost sight of him. Again!

"Shit!"

Over the radio, I announced, "The red car was last seen is in the area of Maple St. But I've lost him!"

Mobile units scrambled. We searched every side street—one car headed to the entrance ramp to the interstate.

After thirty minutes of searching, it was clear that Perez had escaped. Ortiz had no such luck.

The Greek and ATF Agent Moran sat in the front seat of Jack's ATF car. In the backseat, Jason Ortiz was in handcuffs. A .50 caliber Desert Eagle and Tec 9 assault pistol, along with hundreds of rounds of ammunition, were on the car's floor.

As Ortiz was booked at the local P.D., I was still trying to find the red Camaro, but he could have been anywhere in the city. With no other ideas of where to look, I returned to the location where I found him the last time.

As I drove down the residential street, I saw no sign of his red Camaro. I parked around the corner, yet again. I waited. Hours passed. As it was getting dark, I could see the lights going on inside the house. Occasionally I saw a woman, likely his wife, pass by a window.

Patrick Burns

I checked my watch. By now, all other teams were long gone, back at their homes in the Boston area. But I couldn't leave. I needed to find this guy. Finally, at 11:00 p.m., it was clear he would not return home. With nothing to lose, I approached the front door and knocked

A moment later, a thin, pale woman nervously answered the door.

"Yes?" she answered through the crack of the slightly open door.

"I'm looking for your husband. Where's Ralph?"

"He's not here. I don't know where he is," she said, trying to close the door.

There was absolutely no way she didn't know what is going on.

"That's fine, lady," I said with my foot jammed in the door. "I'll go back outside. And I'll just park out in front of your house.

"Sooner or later, I'll find him. And when I do, he's going to jail for a very long time. But you can make it easier on yourself and him if you just let me in to look around. If he's not here, I'll leave."

Looking back, I realized how foolish this was. Alone in a place that no one in the office knew I was at, searching for an armed, desperate drug addict. But at the moment, that wisdom simply didn't cross my mind. I was still in the moment of a hot pursuit chase.

She relented, but after searching the home for weapons and her husband, I found neither. That meant the dozen firearms he purchased recently were all on the street.

"Okay, Mrs. Perez. I believe you. He's not here. I'll go now. But when your husband calls to ask if it's safe to come home, give him a message for me." I handed her my business card.

"What's the message?"

"He has twenty-four hours to call me if he wants to help himself. I want to get some of the guns back off the street. If he doesn't help me, he's going to go to federal prison for a very, very long time."

"Okay. I'll tell him if I see him."

"If? If you see him? Lady, we both know you're going to call him the moment I leave. Listen to me. After 24 hours, all the bad guys in town will know that I was here. Ralph will become useless in trying to recover any of his guns. If you want your husband to improve his jail situation. Have him call me."

"OK."

"The clock is ticking. Twenty-four hours!"

7 *What's a Little Vomit Between Friends?*

After planting the seed with Mrs. Perez, there was nothing more I could do for the time being. As I headed for home, I contemplated my next step. Ralph was on the run. Freaky was on the run from the state and soon will learn about me from Ralph. Except for the two guns we seized from Jason Ortiz, all the others remained on the street, in the hands of dangerous criminals.

I got within a mile from my house. The streets were dark and almost deserted. Suddenly my cell phone rang.

"Hello?"

"Agent Burns? It's Rafael Perez. My wife said you were looking for me?"

"Yes. I am. Where are you?"

"I'm home. Why? Is there a problem? What's this about, sir?"

I smiled to myself. I was in luck; a savvy criminal would never call me. Instead, he'd show up in the morning with a lawyer. He'd claim the 5th. And I'd be empty-handed, with no evidence to hold him.

But Ralph was far from savvy. He seemed to be a foolish optimist, believing he could talk or charm his way out of this. I looked at my watch. It's late, but I can't wait. I can't afford to give him time to disappear, get a lawyer, or warn Freaky.

"Rafael, I want to ask you some questions."

"Sure. No problem, sir. Do you want me to come to your office tomorrow morning?"

"No, I need to talk to you right now. I'm on my way. Don't leave!"

"Now? Here?"

"Yes. Don't go anywhere!"

"OK, sir."

I knew my case was already solid against Perez, and Jason Ortiz, for the Desert Eagle and the Tec 9. But Freaky was still out there somewhere, armed, dangerous, and wanted.

I checked my watch. It was 11:30 PM. The ATF agents who assisted me earlier in the day were back in the Boston area, several hours away. I couldn't expect them to return. Even if they agreed to return, I don't have another approved OP Plan. So I was back to doing this on my own.

As I headed back to the city, I thought about how foolish it was for me to go to Perez's house alone. It was too dangerous. Perez and his clients are all desperate and armed. In the heat of the chase, I did it anyway. But now, with a cooler head as I drove back to the city, I decided I would not make that mistake a second time.

As I pulled over to the side of the road to turn my car around. I dialed the Detective Bureau of the P.D. and was forwarded to the officer in charge of the midnight to eight shift, a.k.a., the Dog Watch. He said he would assign one of his detectives to assist. Great!

Minutes later, as I entered the second-floor detectives' area, I was confronted with several rows of old, banged-up, and bare metal empty desks. Two officers stood in the otherwise deserted, large, open room. All the others were on the street.

The supervisor and Officer Rick Ortiz had been waiting. Turns out, Ortiz had also been searching for Freaky Ti regarding the outstanding warrant for the state charges.

After handshakes and introductions, we grabbed a couple of chairs at vacant desks. Over Officer Ortiz's shoulder, I saw a poster of Starsky & Hutch, the famed detectives on the television show. It was taped up on the window covering a bullet hole. The meeting was short. Within a few minutes, Ortiz and I were on our way out the door to meet Perez.

It's only a ten-minute drive to the other side of town, so we had a little bit of time to discuss our strategy. As we weaved our way through the dark, ghostly streets strewn with garbage, graffiti, burned down houses, and vacant lots, we laid out our approach.

"I don't have an arrest warrant for Perez," I informed Ortiz. "If we get to the house, he could have changed his mind and refuse to talk to us. If that happens, we'll need to leave until I get a warrant."

"OK."

But if that happens, we'll lose our shot at finding Freaky and the 9mm."

Ortiz nodded, indicating no further explanation was needed.

"When Perez called me earlier, he seemed to be optimistically thinking that he would charm his way out of this. He seemed to be trying to give me the impression that it's just a misunderstanding. We'll let him start with that."

"Got it."

"But I don't plan on leaving without finding Freaky and that gun."

"Got it."

As we continued to wind our way through the neighborhoods, we passed through the north end of town. Inside one of the multi-family units, curtains fluttered in through an open window. Inside, two young

Hispanic men were relaxing with the evening breeze, a cold bottle of Colt.45, and a large marijuana cigarette, aka a blunt. Salsa music played in the background as the landlady downstairs cooked rice and beans.

As the man lying on the bed finished taking a puff off the blunt, he grabbed the bottle. Next to it on the table was an overflowing ashtray and a 9mm pistol. As he handed the blunt to the other man, a tattoo on his arm faced upward, "Freaky Ti."

Moments later, Ortiz and I arrived on Perez's street. I noticed the red Camaro was in the driveway. As we pulled up, Raphael and his wife continued to argue about which strategy to use to get out of this mess. But their brainstorming was cut short as they heard our car pull up.

"I've done this many times before, and it's always the same," I said to Officer Ortiz as we sit in the car for a moment before going in. "I'll ask where the 9mm is, knowing it's already on the street and therefore he can't produce it. He will then reply that the gun or guns are kept somewhere else. He'll provide some bogus reason for this. Then I'll ask where exactly? He'll reply, 'at a friend's house' or some similar place."

As Ortiz and I stepped up to the door, it swung open. Sweating and shaking, Ralph Perez mustered the most charming smile he can manage.

"I'm Agent Burns. This is Detective Ortiz. Can we come in?"

"Yes, come in." Ortiz and I shared a glance as we recognize his drug withdrawal symptoms -- trembling, sweating, runny nose.

As we all took a seat at his kitchen table, his wife watched from the next room.

"What can I do for you, agent?" Perez said. "My wife said you wanted to speak to me?"

He was continuing to put forth his best effort to appear helpful and charming. Perhaps he believed I had forgotten about the high-speed chase earlier in the day.

"Where are your guns?"

"Which guns? I, ah, I ah, did have some guns, but I sold them already."

"Where's the 9mm you bought the other day? You bought it last week and already sold it?" I looked him squarely in the eye and leaned forward, showing him I'm not buying this explanation and already losing patience.

"Oh. The 9mm. Ah, that one's ah, that's at a friend's house."

"Why is it at a friend's house and not here?"

"Because of my son. I don't want to have a gun in the house with him here."

"OK. So what's this friend's name who has your 9mm?"

"His first name is Frank. I don't know his last name." Perez replied while we all remain seated at the kitchen table. Ortiz kept an eye out for the wife or anyone else who may step in from the shadows.

"He's a friend you trust with your gun, but you don't know his last name? Okay. So, where does your friend live?"

"In Springfield."

"What's his address?"

"I don't know the, you know, the formal address," Perez said while wiping some sweat from his forehead. "But I can get it for you in the morning, no problem."

"Get your coat."

"What? Why?"

"We're going to see your friend, Frank."

"But ah, it's nighttime...It's best if I go in the morning...." Perez pleaded.

He feared what would happen if he refused us. And what he feared almost as much was Freaky retaliating against him. He was between a rock and a hard place, with no wiggle room.

"Listen to me, Ralph. We can arrest you now. RIGHT NOW. Or you can take us to this so-called friend's house."

Perez sheepishly relented as he grabbed his coat.

It was after midnight as Rafael nervously directed us through a maze of dark, city side streets on our way to find Freaky.

"That's his room right there," Perez pointed up to a second-floor window. The room was lit, and the window was open. We could see curtains blowing into the room.

"Don't get out of this car!" I ordered.

At the front door, Ortiz knocked. We listened. We could vaguely hear muffled sounds on the other side of the door, like people whispering and scattering. But there was no answer at the door.

Beyond our view, one tenant peeked out of a darkened window on the second floor and saw our car out front. Freaky ran downstairs, holding his 9mm in one hand. He found the landlady in the kitchen. Using the gun like a finger, he presses the barrel up against his lips to imply she's not to utter a word. He then shut off her salsa music on the radio and confronted her.

Patrick Burns

"No abras la puerta! Don't open the door!" he whispered before rushing back up the staircase to the second floor, disappearing at the top of the stairs.

Several minutes passed. The landlady sat motionless, nervously waiting in the kitchen, hoping we would simply go away and hoping there won't be gunfire. Freaky Ti stood at a window using the pistol to push back the curtain. He moved it just far enough to peek out and see Perez in the back seat of our car, a car he recognized instantly as an unmarked police car.

"Dumb bitch brought the cops!" Freaky said to the other tenant of the house.

They both exited Freaky's room. After he locked the door, they rushed to the other man's nearby room. Freaky shut off the light as they entered. Then he dove behind the bed and took aim, resting his gun on the top of the mattress. The barrel was pointed directly at the lighted doorway. From this angle, he could see the top of the stairs and shoot anyone who enters the room.

The other man hid in the closet and crouched down on the floor, hoping that if any bullets came his way, they would go over his head.

Ortiz knocked again, moments ticked by. I knocked and yelled, "Police! Open the door! We're not leaving until you open the door!"

Finally, the Hispanic landlady opened the door. But she left the chain lock on and peeked between the crack.

"Policia. I'm looking for Frank Jimenez. I know he lives here," I told her.

"No aqui. He no here," she replied and then tried to close the door.

I knocked again before it closed. "I want to search his room."

"He no here," she replied again.

"Abre la puerta!" Ortiz demanded.

She was still unmoved.

"Listen, lady. You need to let us in, or I'll leave Officer Ortiz here on your front step while I get a federal search warrant. One way or another, we're coming in!"

The woman reluctantly opened the door and stepped back.

"He room es upstairs," she said in broken English while pointing to the lit staircase directly in front of the entrance.

"Vamos por favor," Ortiz told her. "You come with us. Show us."

Looking down at the floor, she reluctantly shuffled her feet to the stairs, like a person walking down death

114

row. Ortiz and I follow the little woman up one flight of the stairs to the second floor.

As we reached the top step, Freaky, still crouched down in the darkened room with his gun aimed in our direction, cocked the 9mm. Ortiz and I were busy speaking to the woman, asking her to direct us to Freaky's room.

"Aqui," she replied as she pointed to a room at the end of the short hallway. We passed by the first room, not knowing we were in the sights of the 9mm.

The woman continued leading us down the hall, never looking up.

"What's in that first room?" I asked.

"Es mi hijo. Es mi son room. He no here."

A moment later, we arrived at the door at the end of the hall.

"This is his room?"

"Si."

I try the door handle. It was locked.

"Open it."

"No puedo. Eezz locked," she said, shrugging her shoulders as if there was nothing more she could do.

"Where's the key?" I asked. She gave me a puzzled look but said nothing.

"Agui esta la llave?" Ortiz asked her.

"Yo no se!"

"Open it now, or we will stay here all night," I told her.

"Momento," she replied and then shuffled toward the stairs to retrieve a butter knife.

As she did, Freaky remained behind the bed in the other room with his gun trained on the doorway. The man hiding in the closet covered his mouth as he fought the sudden urge to vomit. He sensed that the worst could happen at any moment.

Moments later, she returned with the knife.

In just a few more seconds, the door slid open. A cloud of pot smoke escaped into the hallway over our heads. As we drew our weapons, the woman steps out of the way and puts her hands over her ears. But the room was empty.

The room was small, and it only took a few minutes to search it. Freaky and the gun weren't there.

But there was an aroma of pot in the air and an empty pistol case on the table. Freaky was here just moments ago and is likely armed. As I continue to search the room, the landlady remained standing in the doorway. But she kept turning her attention to the hallway. Ortiz watched her.

"What's in that other room?" he asked her.

"Nada. Nada," she replied, but as she did, she kept looking down at the floor, avoiding eye contact with him.

"Let's go," Ortiz told her as he grabs her by the arm. "Take us to that room. Vamos!"

The closer we got to the open door, the more slowly her pace became. She didn't want to go to that room. Something was about to happen. Eventually, she stopped walking altogether. Once she reached a few inches before the door, she refused to take another step.

Ortiz and I shared a glance. Something in that room posed a danger.

Ortiz stepped into the edge of the doorway; I stepped to the other side of the door. Both of us had our weapons aimed around the door frame, into the darkness. I could see nothing. A split-second later, I heard mattress springs moving. Another half-second after that, as my eyes adjusted to the lighting, I could see a silhouette. Someone was on top of the bed.

"Frank. Drop the gun. NOW! Or we'll shoot!" Ortiz yelled as we both aimed our pistols at the shadowy figure on the other side of the bed.

Suddenly, the closet door burst open. An unarmed man ran out, eyes wide, one hand in the air, the other covering his mouth as he tried to hold back the urge to vomit. As he ran by the bed, Freaky dropped the gun onto the covers and then slowly stood up with his hands in the air.

A moment later, we leaned Freaky up against the railing at the top of the staircase. As we snapped the second cuff on his wrist, Perez came running up the stairs, wide-eyed and huffing, eager to see what was happening. The moment he reached the top of the stairs, the terrified man from the closet folded over at the waist, just as his projectile vomit splashed the floor between us.

8   *He Needs Two Shots in the Head*

The next morning, while Freaky and Rafael sat in separate holding cells at the U.S. Marshals' office awaiting arraignment before a federal judge, I was busy attending another funeral.

As before, the death was sudden and unexpected. I learned of it early that morning as I was sitting at the picnic table on my back deck, having a second cup of coffee.

"Dad! The rabbit is laying down!" I'd heard Patrick Jr., my six-year-old son, yell in a voice that sounded very animated and distressed.

A second later, he ran up to my side, looking anxious and gasping for breath. He'd just run up a flight of stairs from the basement. I had my routine each morning, a cup of coffee on the deck. He would go to the basement to feed and play with his ever-growing population of rodents.

"It's early, buddy. She's probably sleeping."

"No, dad. She's laying d o w n," he said, drawing out the word, outstretching both arms like a referee in a boxing match to announce the knockout.

"Laying *down*?" I asked.

"Yes. D O W N!" he replied

"You mean like Spike was lying *down?*" I ask, realizing he means lying flat. Lifeless. Stiff as a board. *That* lying down.

He nodded.

I followed him to the basement storage room, filled with cages holding various guinea pigs, small tunnels, and tiny homes. Next to the cages were bales of hay and a large sack of food pellets.

What had started as a single cage, with one small guinea pig and a small bag of feed, had evolved into more than a dozen rodents, in several enclosures, with multiple homes.

One cage was no longer enough. Guinea pigs are sex machines and get very jealous of who dates their partners. Fights over mates became severe. We had to monitor conflicts and arrange housing according to which pigs got along with each other.

Next to the cages were stacked bales of hay. As the population grew, it became too expensive to buy small bags of hay. Now we purchased full-sized bales from the nearby farm. And we also now needed the twenty-five-pound bag of pellets. What began as one quiet, cuddly pet became a small zoo of fighting, screwing, pooping, and jealous rodents stinking up the entire basement.

Patrick Burns

It was getting out of control. The end of the movie, *Jurassic Park,* was flashing in my mind, the part where the dinosaurs took over.

Anyway, as Patrick led me to the cage housing the black rabbit and her partner, a guinea pig named White Foot, we saw her. She was laid out flat like a miniature bear rug. When I picked her up, she was as stiff as a board.

So it was back to the pine tree for a second impromptu funeral.

After the burial, I headed downtown to the Springfield P.D. They'd provided a back-up detective on the Perez/Freaky arrests. Now it was time for me to return the favor.

A little bit earlier that morning, at 8:00 AM, a call came into the Detective Division. Captain Noonan took the call from Parole Officer Eric Mawhinney.

"Good morning Eric. What can I do for you today?"

"Good morning, Bill. I've got one of my parolees here in my office. He's shitting his pants right now. Seems he stumbled into a murder-for-hire plot, or so he says. He says he'd been chatting with a woman online, on one of the local dating sites. According to him, she tried to hire him to kill her husband. So he's here now and wants to report the solicitation, just to make sure he doesn't get caught up in it as an accessory to murder or something like that."

"Is the husband already dead?"

"No. I don't think so. But that could happen at any moment. The woman told my guy she wants him killed by the weekend."

"That's in just three days! Why then?"

"It's the end of the month. Food stamps come out on the first. She wants it done before then so she can get a full month of his food stamps allocation next month. His W.I.C. card will get credited on the first."

"She wants to kill him for $100 in food stamps?" Noonan asked.

"That's what it sounds like," Mawhinney replied, "Go figure.".

"Okay, what's this woman's name?" Noonan grabs a pen and pad.

Eric looks up from the speakerphone to ask the parolee. He's seated across the desk, shuffling his feet, wringing his hands on the edge of his chair.

"What's her name?"

He comes back to the phone.

"Bill, he said he doesn't know her real name. But he said her screen name is "Kiki." That's all he knows. …Oh, and she gave him a picture of herself and her husband. Poor bastard has no idea his wife is trying to whack him. Anyway, I'll just send this guy over to your office so you can take it from here."

"Thanks, Eric," Noonan hung up the phone.

At 10:00 AM, I arrived at the detectives' squad room. Captain Bill Noonan, Corporal Sean Condon, and State Trooper Norman Shink, the team known as Starsky and Hutch, were all waiting. We sat down in the large, otherwise empty squad room to discuss our strategy.

"Okay, we need to talk to this guy and find out exactly what happened. That's number one. And no matter what this parolee *says* happened, we need to find out for ourselves.

"We can't do anything at all based solely on this guy's word. He's a felon and on parole. No jury will believe his word over hers, nor should they. This guy has made the entire thing up to gain points with his Parole Officer for all we know. We need to develop the evidence independently."

Everyone nodded in agreement.

"And we need to do it fast before she does have him killed. We only have three days."

"Should we alert the victim?" one officer asked.

"No. As of now, we don't even know if any of this is true. And even if it were true, it would kill our chance of preventing the murder and arresting her. The victim would immediately tell the wife. She'd call it off, for now at least.

"But she could just wait a week or month and do it when we were not able to keep an eye on her. It could be made to look like a robbery gone bad. And she'd likely get away with it. So no, we don't tell the husband, for now. He'll be safer in the long run if we can just get her off the street first."

"So what's the plan?" asked one officer.

"We get this guy, the parolee, to cooperate with us. We get him to bring up the subject with her. Get the words coming directly from her mouth. But she has to specifically say that she wants the husband killed. And it needs to be on tape if we're going to convince a jury.

"The problem is," the Captain continued, "our liberal Massachusetts laws are designed to protect the criminals, not the victims. We would practically need the Governor to approve monitoring and recording her conversations.

"And even if we could get the blessing, it would take weeks, if not months. She wants him dead by the weekend. We don't have months; we have three days. The victim would be dead before we ever got approval."

"At the federal level, I can get approval in just a few hours," I said.

"Yes. Exactly. And that's why we invited you in."

Officer Condon stepped forward. "And this just came up on our system," handing me a report of a domestic disturbance call. "We have a phone number and a possible address for Kiki."

The report, dated last fall, says a woman called 911 to report an assault by her husband. The phone number on the 911 call is listed to a Kristi Jarvis, at an address in one of the local subsidized housing projects.

"Looks like this "Kiki" is Kristi Jarvis," the captain said.

"I agree," I said. "We can get approval to record the conversations. But like you said, we'll need that parolee to cooperate. He's the one she's been talking to. We need him to accept to do the murder at her direction and get it all on tape."

"Agreed," Captain Noonan said. "We have only three days to make this happen. So let's move."

***

As we waited for approval for the operation, a few miles away, on the outskirt of the city, Kiki wasn't waiting for anything. She was right back at it, busy chatting online, trying to seduce another prospective killer. The interview took place at her cluttered kitchen table. Facing the screen on her laptop computer, she giggled and flirted with a promising candidate.

The interview was interrupted by noisy kids. Behind Kiki, in the subsidized housing unit she shared with her husband, their three young children competed for her attention. The infant cried as she struggled to get untangled from a pile of clothes. The other two toddlers took turns whining and demanding snacks.

"Yes, baby. I'm still here. Yes. I'll send you a picture of me, honey. I hope you like it," she replies with a flirty giggle.

She clicked on the file of a wallet-sized picture of herself and her husband, Mathew Moore, then hit the "send" key. Instantly, an image appears on the prospect's computer screen. He viewed the picture of a younger, thinner Kiki, likely taken years ago. In it, her pasty white skin is in stark contrast with that of her black husband.

He's strikingly handsome and fashionably dressed, wearing a designer sweater, a large gold necklace, and gold earrings. His hair perfectly groomed, right down to the shine from hair gel.

Patrick Burns

As she waited to know if the candidate liked her picture, Kiki walked to the front window to look outside. The front lawn was dirt, without a speck of grass. On the street, nothing except her broken-down Mitsubishi. It had been parked there for several months.

Finally, she heard an incoming message. The man on the other end of the chat has sent a reply. "I see the picture. You look great, baby! I'd like to have you right now!"

"Me too, honey," Kiki replies with a giggle, typing into the chatbox. "Me, too."

"Is your husband there with you now?" he asked.

"No, silly. He's at work. But if you want me, you need to get him out of my life first. Then we can be together."

"Out of your life, how?"

"Are you a bad boy?"

"Am I a "Bad boy?"

"Yes, silly." She giggled. "Have you ever been to jail?"

"Yes. I've been to jail. Why?"

"Then I may have a job for you. That's why."

"What job is that?"

"Well, I don't trust this chat line, baby. Someone could be listening. What's your phone number? We can talk on the phone. It's safer."

As Kiki continued her conversation over the telephone, our team continued waiting for approval. Finally, at 4 PM, I get the call. Assistant United States Attorney (AUSA) Paul Smyth is on the line.

"Judge Ponser has signed off. You guys are all set. Good luck!"

***

Within an hour, Starsky, Hutch, and I were with the parolee, Davon Washington, parked at the end of a deserted street in an empty section of town and concealed in my tinted-out, unmarked ATF car. Starsky had a tape recorder, and we were almost ready to make our first call to Kiki.

Trooper Shink, aka Starsky, was seated in the passenger seat, putting a set of new double A batteries into our tape recorder. Condon was in the rear seat with the informant.

"I just want you guys to know I'm not a killer," Devon asserted. "I'm a petty thief. That's all. You can check my record."

"We know that, Davon," I said. "You won't have any problems with this. But before you call Kiki, we need to know exactly what happened between you the last time you spoke to her. Exactly what was said? This next conversation needs to make sense to her."

"Okay. Well, I met her online. We chatted for a while. On our second chat, she told me she'd like to meet me, but she was married. I said, you know, that's cool. And then she told me if I wanted her, she would be interested and all. But I'd need to get rid of her husband first. I thought, you know, maybe she meant that she wanted me to threaten him or something."

"Then what? Did you meet her in person?"

"Yeah. The next day we met on the street. She gave me this picture."

Davon handed Condon a wallet-size picture of Kiki and her husband.

"What else did she say?"

"She said, "I hope you like my picture. That's my husband next to me in it.""

"And then?"

"I asked if she wanted to come over to my place. She said "yes," but first, I need to 'off' her husband. So now I'm thinking, hold on. Then she tells me she wants it done by Friday."

"Okay," I said. "Here's what you need to do. Call her and ask if she still wants you to get rid of her husband.

But we can't simply leave it at that. You need to ask her exactly what she wants you to do and how to do it.

"That's number one.

"Also, you need to tell her that killing her husband is going to be a two-man job. You have a partner. So that's number two. Three is telling her it will cost her $2,000, $1,000 for you, and $1,000 for your partner."

Shink was seated in the passenger seat, and he handed the tape recorder to Condon. Condon attaches it to the informant's cell phone, and Davon dialed the number to Kiki's apartment.

"Hi, Kiki. It's me," Davon told her as he held the cell phone to his ear, a wire dangling from it to the attached tape recorder.

"Hi, baby. I miss you. When will you do it, baby?"

"When will I do what?"

"You know, get rid of him, honey."

Still seated behind the steering wheel in the driver's seat, I grabbed a pen and a three by five index card. I hold it up for Davon's view. It says, "SHOOT HIM!"

"Oh. Right. How do you want me to do it? Do you want me to shoot him once in the head?"

"No, honey, he needs *TWO SHOTS* to the head!" She giggles as if the thought of two shots in her husband's head amused her.

Needing to maintain silence, I said nothing, but I gave him the "thumbs up."

"Okay. I can do that. Is there anything else?"

"Yes. I want it to look like a robbery. You can do it when he leaves work. He works the second shift at H&D packaging in Hartford. He finishes work at midnight. I can show you where he works and where he parks his car. You just need to wait for him near his car."

Kiki didn't know it, but by adding a trip across state lines from Massachusetts to Connecticut into her plan, this has just become a federal murder case. Again, I gave the informant the "thumbs up."

"Okay, I can do that," the informant said.

I next jotted down a note. Then I held up another index card that said: "PAYMENT = $2,000". After he read it, I immediately held up another card, TWO-MAN JOB, PARTNER.

He told Kiki.

"But I don't have $2,000, my love."

The informant looked to us, shrugging his shoulders... I jot down, "SOMETHING WORTH $2,000?"

"No. I'm broke. I can't even afford to fix my car. It doesn't run. That's why I need his car after you kill him."

"You have a car?"

"Yes, a Mitsubishi. But it doesn't start."

I hold up another card. "PARTNER HAS A TOW TRUCK."

"It's okay. My partner has a tow truck. It's cool. We'll take the Mitsubishi as payment."

The conversation continued a little longer. Kiki agreed to the terms. She confirmed that she wanted the husband killed by two shots to the head. She wanted it to look like a robbery. She wanted it done by the weekend at his place of employment in Connecticut.

"Okay, honey. So when will you do it?"

"My partner and I will pick up the car tomorrow, and then you can show us where your husband works and where he parks his car."

"I can't wait, honey! After you do it, we can be together. Should I call the police and say I'm worried because my husband didn't come home from work?" her tone giddy and getting more excited by the minute. "I can cry and act all scared like I'm worried something happened to him!"

"No. Just let them call you after it's done."

"Okay. And I'll act surprised and cry, like, 'Oh my God! Oh my God!'"

"Yeah. You do that."

Starsky, Hutch, and I all gave the informant the thumbs up. He told Kiki he'd see her tomorrow afternoon and hung up the phone.

I next called ATF Boston, Division Headquarters, to request an undercover ATF agent to pose as Davon's partner for the murder. I also asked for an undercover vehicle wired for sound and video. And finally, I requested a back-up team.

We needed to show a jury Kiki was serious and willing to go through with it. But her car not running posed a problem as to her paying for the hit. Fortunately, one of the area's most prominent tow truck companies is owned by a retired Springfield police officer. Steve, the Greek, knew him personally and arranged to get an undercover tow truck. And to drive it, there was no officer more suited to look like a tow truck driver than the Greek himself. His beard, his handlebar mustache, and his tattered and dandruff covered sweater made him the perfect fit.

***

The next day, a Friday afternoon, Kristi Jarvis, a.k.a. Kiki, watched out the living room window as a tow truck pulled up to the curb in front of her home. It stops one car length ahead of the broken-down green Mitsubishi. A few seconds later, she watched a barrel-chested man with a long, gray handlebar mustache climb down from the driver's seat.

Officer Steve Maurangadakis, a.k.a. The Greek, wearing a T-shirt with the logo matching the tow truck company on the truck door, approached the home of Kristi Jarvis. He knocked.

Instantly, the door swung open, and he saw a short, smiling white woman. He recognized her as Kristi from the photo she provided to the informant.

"I'm here for the car," he said as he handed her a towing authorization slip. "Sign it on the bottom line."

Kiki grabbed his pen and didn't hesitate. She signed the authorization form and used her real name.

"Follow me," Steve said as he tucked the receipt in his pocket and led her to the truck.

It's now available as evidence. The signed authorizing is the equivalent of a signed check, proof of payment for the murder.

"Are you ready? I'll bring you to my partner's car. It's around the corner. Hop in. You don't want him to be seen here at your house," the Greek told her as Kiki climbs up into his tow truck.

Patrick Burns

Within five minutes, they arrived at a nearby parking lot. The Greek, on cue, pulled the tow truck into an empty space next to a gray four-door sedan. ATF Agent Thurman—a large, linebacker-sized black man behind the wheel of the undercover vehicle—gave the Greek a nod and then reached under the dashboard. He flipped a hidden switch, and instantly, the audio recorder came on.

Seated next to Tony in the front passenger seat was our informant. In the rear seating area, directly behind Tony, was a pile of dirty clothes, leaving only one spot for Kiki to sit. She hopped in right behind Davon and right in front of the hidden camera lens.

Tony hit a second switch under the dashboard. The camera started recording.

"All set?" Davon asked Jarvis.

Kiki smiled and nodded, looking like a child eager for Christmas to arrive.

"This is my partner for the job," Davon said, introducing Agent Thurman by his undercover name. "Which way do we go?"

"His company is Exit 41 in Connecticut. Just get on Interstate 91 and head south. I'll show you where he parks his car," Kiki giggled, animated and giddy.

Moments later, as the would-be killers headed for the on-ramp to Interstate 91, I was alone in a separate car following loosely behind them. Other surveillance units leapfrogged up and down as they maintained a roving perimeter on the highway. Agent Thurman engaged the target in conversation as they traveled. I listened in with my two-way radio and updated the roving units as we go.

"All units," I said, "we're approaching the Dunkin Donuts at the bottom of the highway ramp."

"I see you," Condon replied from his marked police cruiser tucked behind the building.

Thurman steered toward the south lane on Route 91. I continued to follow three cars behind.

It was a 30-minute trip. Thurman continued talking with Kiki, asking where to drive and how she wanted the husband killed.

The roving units and I continued at a short distance behind them. Finally, I spotted what was needed to turn this state murder-for-hire prosecution into a federal case, the highway sign "Welcome to Connecticut."

As we passed it, Kiki didn't know she was now about to face federal prison. But the ride wasn't over – she still has time to back out of this and save herself and her husband.

"Keep going. It's a few more exits," Kiki told the driver as they continued south.

Patrick Burns

A few minutes later, they reached the food processing center. She pointed out the parking spot where her husband parked his car each night.

"He'll be getting out at midnight. That's his car right there, the brown car. He'll be leaving out that door," she added, pointing to an unmarked exit door.

"Got it."

"It should look like a robbery," she said. "You keep the cash and necklace. I'll get his car."

As this was happening, I was a half-mile away in my separate car, listening.

"So in the morning, I should call the police to say my husband is missing … and act all worried, right?

"Sure. You do that," Thurman said as he steered the car onto the ramp heading north, back to Massachusetts.

Moments later, Thurman's cell phone rang. "Hello?"

"Tony, it's me. I'm losing the conversation transmission. Did she show you the parking slot?"

"Sure. Yeah. We're good."

"Has she said she changed her mind?"

"Nope. But we'll see. Catch you later."

Using the rearview mirror, Tony looked Kiki in the eyes.

"Kiki, let me ask you. How many children do you have with our husband?"

"We have three."

"What ages are they?"

"Three, two, and one."

"Wow. Are you sure you want to kill the father of your young children?"

"Oh, yes. I'm sure. I tried to kill him myself, but I couldn't do it.

"You tried yourself? How did you do that?"

"Yeah. He was sleeping. I got a brick from the front yard. I stood over him on the bed and smashed it over his head."

"Then what happened?"

"He woke up crying. He asked me why I did it, and then he ran out of the house! I told him it was a ghost that did it."

Thurman had no reply and turned his attention back toward the road.

Patrick Burns

Moments later, they approached the off-ramp back in Springfield. I dialed Thurman's phone number.

"Tony, this is it. We're minutes away from the take-down site. Did she change her mind?"

This was the final moment where she could have walked away from this.

"Hell no. Not at all."

"So, we're good to make the arrest?"

"Correct. It won't be long. I'm hitting all the green lights," Thurman replied, stating the code words "green light" as meaning to proceed with the arrest.

"So she didn't call it off?" I asked again to be sure.

"That's right. It's a green light."

As Thurman, Kiki, and the informant were about to drive passed the Dunkin Donuts, Condon pulled his cruiser out from behind its concealment and turned onto the road, inches from their rear bumper.

Tony looked in his rearview mirror and sees flashing blue lights. Thurman flipped on his directional signal and pulls the car into the Dunkin Donuts parking lot.

This was it. Kiki expressed an intent to commit murder. Now we had other concerns. When she got into the car, she wasn't patted-down for a weapon. That would have been impractical. As she sat in the rear seat, we didn't know if she was armed, so the best approach was to take the agent and the informant out before we laid hands on her.

"License and registration, please," Condon demanded while standing at Tony's window.

"I don't have a license," Thurman replied on cue.

"Please step out of the car, sir," Condon demands.

As Kiki's attention is drawn to watching the officer interacting with her hired hitman, I already parked my car in the donut shop nearby and walk over.

"Please step out of the car, Kristi," I said as I opened her rear door. "You're under arrest for interstate travel to commit murder."

Frozen, seemingly in shock, she glanced up at me with sad puppy eyes. Her giddy, giggling optimism has evaporated as she slowly stepped out. I helped her get up and gently applied handcuffs. Next stop, downtown.

***

Months afterward, in Federal District Court, Kristi Jarvis was seated silently at the defendant table with her court-appointed lawyer. At the prosecution table, I was sitting next to Assistant U.S. Attorney Paul Smyth. A few family members were in the spectator benches, including her husband, Mathew Moore.

Patrick Burns

At the direction of the Judge, Kristi nervously rose to her feet, hands folded in front of her.

"Are you entering a plea of guilty in this matter?" the judge asks.

Her answer is barely a whisper, "Yes."

"I accept your plea of guilty," the judge says, banging his gavel. "You may be seated."

Kristi Jarvis received eight years in federal prison for hiring assassins to travel interstate to kill her husband.

As AUSA Smyth and I stepped onto the elevator to head down to the ground level, Moore stepped in behind us.

Moore and I hadn't met. But since he was the victim of a federal crime, Smyth had notified him of the court date and met him personally before we went in.

"Mr. Moore. Have you met Agent Burns?" Smyth asks as the elevator descends.

"No," he replied, a bit subdued.

"Well," Smyth said, looking Moore in the eye and tilting his head toward me. "This is Agent Burns. You might want to thank him. He just saved your life."

9   *Coffee Time*

After the court proceeding, it was time to get back to looking for new targets. Each agent finds his or her cases, and finding gun traffickers was the top priority. Second on the priority list are convicted felons with guns.

How to find them is left up to each agent. One place to look is within the information gathered from the daily gun trace requests. Each request sent to ATF from the local departments lists all the weapons seized in local crimes.

The requests are a good starting point. If the trace links several guns used to commit crimes to one common buyer, that person would be worth looking into.

Besides the gun trace reports, local gun shop owners are another source for leads, as seen in the Perez case.

When those two sources don't produce enough leads, hitting the streets searching for targets can also produce results. It helps to have good relationships with local police officers.

In my situation, that officer was Sean Condon.

The only problem was, ATF considered patrolling to be surveillance and surveillance to be an enforcement action. After the disastrous outcome of ATF's attempt to arrest Branch Davidian leader David Koresh, resulting in the deaths of eighty people, including innocent children, the agency instituted very restrictive rules governing the use of enforcement actions.

Those rules required all agents to prepare an Operational Plan (OP Plan) before conducting law enforcement operations. But there was no way to get a pre-approved plan for driving around and looking for action.

So Condon and I discovered a solution. Instead of doing surveillance, we'd simply get a coffee.

A few times each week, my cell phone would ring.

"Hi, Pat. It's me, Sean. Do you want to get a coffee?"

If I wasn't busy and needed to find more targets, I'd reply, "Sounds good."

"Great. See you in 10 minutes."

They required no OP Plan to get a cup of coffee. If we drove around for a few hours deciding on which coffee shop to visit, and some criminals fled from our car as we arrived in a neighborhood, or if Sean recognized a fugitive walking down the sidewalk, Oops.

The chase was on, and I had my cases.

On one such afternoon, ten minutes after his call, I looked down from the second-floor window of the federal courthouse as a battle-scarred blue Crown rolled up to the curb. A short, stocky, white-haired former Marine sat behind the wheel.

"Ready?" he asked as I hopped into the passenger seat.

"Yep. Let's go."

There was no coffee in the car, and it was hit or miss if we'd ever find the right place to find one. But on our way, we headed to some of the city's roughest areas, the neighborhoods on Sean's beat. As we slowly rolled through the usual streets, we scanned the faces of pedestrians.

We rolled past the gangsters hanging out on dilapidated front porches. They sized us up as we approached, and we did the same to them. If one had a gun or a good-sized package of dope, it would come down to a game of chicken.

We'd slow near the group and watch their eyes and movements. They watched us and calculated when to run or when to hold.

Sometimes on our "patrols," Sean's dash-mounted computer screen chirped, announcing new incoming alerts/messages. Each time it chirped, the screen would light up with new information regarding crimes inside the city or announcing reminders or look-outs being posted for cars or persons of interest.

Patrick Burns

As Sean continued driving, alternating his focus from the road to the computer, he tapped the screen to read the most recent alert. "1995 Honda Civic, plate GV123 reported stolen from Hollywood section. Color white...." It was not near our area. Sean ignored it and re-focused on the streets. We chatted as he drove.

"So, I heard you were in the Marines, too?"

"Yeah. 1976 Cherry Point." I replied.

"I was at Camp Pendleton for boot camp."

"Parris Island."

Sean paused the conversation to read another incoming report on a stolen Nissan in another section of town.

"So, what's your plan for the weekend?" he asked as he turned the car onto Bay Street.

"I'm going sailing."

"How big is your boat? Does it have a name?"

"It's a 25-footer. I named it 'Fat Chance,'" I replied with a chuckle.

"Fat Chance? Is there a joke in there somewhere?"

"Yes. It's because my wife Eleanor said she didn't want me to buy it. Her exact words were it would be a

'Fat Chance' of me ever owning a sailboat. So I bought it and named it 'Fat Chance.' I laughed.

"That's funny!"

"Oh. There's more. After I owned it for a while, she told me that I was spending too much time on it. She said if I kept sailing on it that she'd divorce me."

"So then what?"

"I told her if she did, I'd rename it, Last Straw."

Just then, the dash-mounted computer chirped again.

"Beep, beep, beep" Sean tapped the screen. "Any units in the area of Bay and Brown Streets, be advised a report of a suspect with a gun at the B&B Convenience Store."

"Condon to dispatch. We're already right there. I'll take it ...over."

He parked a short distance from the store with a clear view of its entrance door.

"We'll set up here and wait to see if he comes out," he said, without looking over at me. His eyes were already fixed on the door of the shop.

Patrick Burns

We waited. So far, no sight of the suspect. As we waited, the dispatcher forwarded the full report to Sean via his car's computer.

I watched the store entrance. The suspect, Gary Curtis, was listed as a known gang member and a fugitive from justice in New York. He was also a convicted felon. That meant Sean and I both had jurisdiction for his arrest. But my dilemma remained. I had no approved OP Plan for an arrest. So if I participated in it and backed Sean up, I'd be violating policy. If something went wrong, I'd be held accountable, tossed instantly under the bus by management.

But allowing Sean to go ahead alone, while I sat in the car, was not an option. If an agent did that, they didn't belong in this line of work. So if we spotted Curtis, I knew it would be game on, one way or another.

The report continued: Curtis was seen moments ago inside the store wearing red and white gym clothes. The caller also spotted a gun tucked in the small of the suspect's back. It was described as a semi-automatic pistol and seemed to have an obliterated serial number.

Watching from our car at the curb, about twenty meters from the B&B Convenience store, we had a clear view of the entrance. So far, there was no sign of him.

"Do you think he left?" I asked.

"Maybe. But let's give it five minutes. If he doesn't show, we'll go inside."

A small group of pedestrians loitered in front of the nearby Face and Nails Salon. Other pedestrians gathered on the street corners. There was light traffic on Bay Street. We continued to watch the door of B&B Convenience. The door was open.

A moment later, a man's arm and leg appeared.

"Here we go!"

The man fitting the suspect's description stood at the threshold, apparently talking with someone inside the store. Sean and I exchanged glances. The clothing matched the description. He was wearing a gym suit; the colors were red and white.

"That's him. Let's go," Condon said as he opened his driver's side door and stepped into the street, his eyes never leaving the suspect.

I stepped out of the passenger side and onto the sidewalk. Then we cautiously approached without a word. When we were a few meters from the door, Curtis stepped outside.

"Yo, buddy," Condon said, now looking up as he stood next to the line-backer sized man. I moved to flank him.

Patrick Burns

Curtis looked down at Sean's face. He glanced next at Condon's duty belt, adorned with two sets of chrome handcuffs and a.40 caliber pistol. Curtis' eyes instantly snapped up to look around, searching for an escape route.

Without a word, the large man pivoted on his heels and positioned his feet to take off running. Condon instantly grabbed hold of the man's shirt sleeve.

For an instant, the man was stuck, as Condon held tightly onto his clothing. But that ended quickly as Curtis bent over at the waist, slipping out of the shirt. As Condon held on, the man wiggled further out of the shirt, exposing his naked back, and the pistol up against it, tucked in his waistband.

There was no time for thoughts of danger to enter my mind. Instinct and training took over. I was on autopilot.

It was not my ATF training that took over. It was my high school training. I'd been on the wrestling team for four years. I'd spent thousands of hours, seven days per week drilling and grappling. One drill we had spent countless hours practicing was a whistle drill. A whistle was blown, and each wrestler's reaction time was tested.

When I saw that gun in Curtis' waistband, it was like someone blew a whistle. I reacted instinctively, in a fraction of a second. I charged him. I wrapped my arms around his torso and attempted to take him down to the ground. But he was too big and strong. Instead, we remained standing in the middle of Bay Street, swaying back and forth, in a bear hug embrace.

As I had my arms wrapped tightly around his upper body, my stomach remained tightly pressing against his back. Suddenly I could feel his gun pressing against me. I realized that he had no way to grab it.

Great!

Back and forth we struggled, him fighting to escape and me struggling to take him to the ground. As the stalemate continued, we gradually drifted toward the other side of the street, away from the store.

For several minutes it went on, like two Greco-Roman wrestlers in an upper-body embrace, each struggling to get a better footing.

Suddenly, I felt my right shoe come off. We shuffled more. But now, I had been reduced to one shoe and one sock for my footing. We struggled more. He was gaining ground, but I was still latched firmly onto him.

Just then, my other shoe came off. And as he struck me, blood dripped down my temple.

When we reached a neighbor's front yard, we continued to fight. Me bloody and in my socks, the criminal still desperately trying to lose me. Again he tried to twist his body to free himself. That's when I felt my hand fall upon his 9mm. Instantly my thumb then brushed against the ejector switch. I pressed it.

"Clang!" I heard the steel magazine clip hit the dirt. That meant he had either an empty gun or only one round remaining in the chamber.

I wrapped my leg around his. "Bam!" We both hit the dirt. He landed face down; I stayed on top of his back. As I looked down, the gun was now sitting right in front of me. I grabbed it and tucked it into my waistband.

He was now disarmed, but my victory wasn't assured. The commotion caught the attention of the neighbors. An angry mob circled us like hyenas. I felt my strength waning. My tunnel vision was fading. I looked up and saw the crowd. From the ground, all I saw was a sea of legs.

"Give me your hands!"

Time was running out. I yelled to Curtis again, my concern for the angry crowd growing. We needed to get out of there soon.

Sirens began to be heard wailing in the distance. Back-up police units raced to the scene from surrounding areas. Moments later, the marked cruisers rolled up. Uniformed officers pushed through the crowd that surrounded us.

My strength was all but gone as I struggled to get handcuffs on him. I had little left. I grabbed my baton to speed things up.

It must have been entertaining to watch, two men on the ground fighting, one on top, covered in blood, swinging a club at the other.

One officer, sensing an imminent riot in the making, ran up to me and grabbed the baton from my hand.

"It's okay, Pat. I'll take it from here."

Another agent stepped through the crowd, leaned down, and grabbed my arm. He said nothing, just led me to an open car door, retrieved a bottle of drinking water, and flushed my wounds.

Several local officers whisked Curtis through the crowd and into one of the marked cruisers' back seat. The car disappeared down Bay Street, headed to the station. Within just a few more minutes, all the remaining agents and officers disbursed in different directions. Then the crowd left. Soon everything returned to normal as if it had never happened.

I never did get my coffee that day.

10   *He's Not a Runner Anymore!*

"Call 911! Get an ambulance!" I yelled toward the darkened, empty second-floor bedroom windows.

It was the middle of winter in Springfield, Massachusetts, at 2:00 a.m. I staggered along my icy driveway in the freezing air. Dressed only in pajamas and wrapped in a blanket, I called out again, hoping someone in my family would hear me.

But there was no response. They were all asleep. I could see my breath each time I gasped for oxygen. As I watched it leave my failing lungs, I hoped the cold air would relax them and allow more oxygen in. But it wasn't working.

What the hell was happening, I wondered as I sat at the picnic table freezing, hoping to hear an ambulance approaching. But there was none. That's when it dawned on me. This wasn't a heart attack. It was a reaction to my son's damn guinea pigs!

An hour earlier, I'd been sleeping peacefully in my bed. Suddenly I woke, fighting for air. It felt like someone had placed a pillow over my face, and I was trying to breathe through it. No matter how much I struggled, I couldn't get air.

Dazed and not knowing what was happening, I'd decided to go outside and try to breathe some cold, fresh air, so I wrapped in a blanket and made my way to the family car. I needed air, and I needed to sleep. I reclined in the front seat.

When that proved useless, I tried to increase my breathing rate to get more oxygen into my lungs. That only led to hyperventilating. Now, seated in the car, I wasn't only gasping for air but also feeling dizzy. The situation was getting worse, not better. It was no use. Finally, I decided to go back inside.

But after stepping back out of the driver's side of the car, I staggered as I walked toward the rear of the house. I made it to the picnic table as the chest pains began.

When he'd first asked to have one guinea pig, I refused. I told him I was very allergic to rodents and cats. But he hounded me relentlessly, day and night, for weeks on end.

Eventually, I gave in. I told him we would try just one pig, and we'd see if my lungs could take it. I figured that even though I was allergic, it would be only one small rodent, and it would be kept far away from me, down in the basement. After we got the first one, Spike, he'd ask every day if I still felt okay.

And at first, I did.

But one pig later led to another and then another, and in the end, we had more than a dozen. It had taken

154

a few months for their dander to saturate the air ducts of the house. But finally, it made its way to my bedroom at 1 a.m. that evening.

As I waited for the ambulance, I thought about the conversation I'd be having with Patrick in the morning. He could keep either the pigs or his dad, but not both.

As rapidly as the symptoms came on, they vanished. The icy cold air had done the trick. The next morning the pigs were on their way to many of Patrick's friends' houses and other wonderful homes.

*****

As the months passed, the home's air quality gradually improved. Fortunately, everything was back to normal; only a few added tombstones decorate the flower bed beneath the pine tree.

It was now the middle of the summer of 2002. All of my active casework and gun tracing administrative work were finished for the day, and it was time to look for more criminals with guns. Like clockwork, after lunch, I received an invitation to go "get a coffee."

By early afternoon Condon and I were cruising through our usual neighborhoods. We were always looking for criminals with active warrants and watching for any suspicious activities leading to finding a criminal with an illegal gun.

So far, all was quiet. We chatted as we rolled up to the corner on Sycamore Street, the turf of the Sycamore Street gang.

"Help! Help!" we heard the scream of a woman. A moment later, she jumped into the road and ran toward the front of our car with hands raised and waving frantically back and forth in the air. Her dress was ripped, and she had a look of horror on her face.

Condon slammed on the breaks just as she fell over the front of our hood, a second away from being run over.

"Please. You need to help me!" she pleaded, gasping to catch her breath.

"Help you do what?" Sean asked her as we stood outside the car with her.

"He robbed and raped me. Oh my God, you gotta catch him. He has my purse! He has everything!" she said as tears came from her eyes.

"Get in!" said Condon.

"Oh, my God! Please, you gotta help me," she cried as she sat in our back seat with hands over her face.

"Who raped you?" Sean asked. "Where is he now?"

"He's one of the neighbors. I don't know his name. I've seen him before. He lives down the street."

"Where is he now?" Condon asked as he shifted the car back into gear and hit the gas.

"I don't know where he lives... I just got out of there. But he's still there!"

"Still where?"

"At my apartment!" she said, composing herself after seeing we would help her.

"Which way?"

"Take a right. It's the greenhouse over there, the second-floor."

A moment later, Condon slammed on the breaks, and the car screeched to a halt on the sidewalk in front of the three-story green apartment building.

"Stay here!" Sean ordered her as we both jumped out of the car.

"Pat, you cover the back!" Sean said as he headed toward the front door.

"Be careful. He's a runner!" the woman yelled to us from the back seat of the police car.

As I reached the back yard, Sean knocked on the front door.

"Police! Open up!" Sean yelled as he hit the front door. His voice carried to the back yard where I was standing. No doubt the man on the second floor could hear him also. But no one came to the door.

"Police! Open up!" Sean yelled again, still no response.

The banging and yelling continued for several minutes. The victim remained in the car while I covered the back door. Then, out of the corner of my eye, I noticed a second-floor window slowly and quietly sliding open. I watched as it reached the top of the track. A moment later, I saw a work boot, then a leg, and then a man slipping out the window onto a short roof above the first-floor porch.

I watched him run across the roof. When he reached the end of the roof, he didn't stop running. He also didn't stop at the edge to hang down to ease his drop. He simply kept running full speed off the edge, his legs still pumping, as he flew in the air toward the asphalt below.

"Bam!" he landed with both feet into the soft asphalt. The hot summer heat had heated it to a thick, sticky paste. As the runner hit the pasty tar, his body continued forward, but his feet remained planted in the spot they'd landed.

"My foot! My foot!" He screamed a moment later.

I had started running in his direction when I saw him on the roof. Seconds after he landed, I was already straddled on his back.

Patrick Burns

Screaming in pain, he continued to yell, "My foot! My foot!"

Evidently, he expected to just hit the ground running like something you'd see in a cartoon.

I looked down at his foot. At first, it appeared that his left boot had come off. But when I looked closer, I realized that the boot hadn't come off. It was lying on the ground next to him, twelve inches away from his ankle, with his foot was still in it. The bone sticking out looked like a chicken bone when you break it from the carcass. The bone and tendons were exposed.

"Give me your hands!" I yelled.

"But my foot, my foot!" He wailed.

"Yeah. I know. Now give me your hands!"

Even with a broken foot, if he was armed, he was still dangerous. There was nothing wrong with his arms. I had no idea if he had a pistol tucked into his waistband. My training guided me to ignore the foot and simply snap on the second handcuff. The paramedics and a Springfield detective approached me. The officer said he'd handle it from there.

As the EMTs took the rapist/ robber to the ER, Condon and I walked back to our car, where the victim had remained patiently in our back seat, watching the show.

"You got him! Thank you. Thank you so much!"

"Yeah," Sean said. "We got him. It's OK. He won't bother you again.... And by the way, he's not a runner anymore!"

11   *The Book Store*

On the outskirts of Springfield, a caravan of unmarked police cars wound its way through an industrial section of town. After navigating through several side streets, the cars and SUVs peeled off from the rest of the city traffic. One-by-one each disappeared behind a large, nondescript four-story commercial building.

Behind it, out of view from the passing traffic, they reassembled in the staging area. Soon, small groups of plain-clothed police officers, state troopers, and federal agents exited the vehicles and filtered into the plush lobby. The groups ascended a flight of thickly carpeted spiral stairs, stopping at an unmarked, locked door at the top.

Hung above it, a clock on the CCTV camera read 9:35 a.m. One man pressed the doorbell as the others patiently stood by. Their image instantly appeared on the other side of the door on a matching monitor. The young receptionist viewed the image, smiled, and then pressed a button concealed under her desk.

Instantly, a second buzzer was heard, along with a metallic clicking sound. The lock on the entrance door snapped open. The visitors filed inside.

Each officer smiled, waved, or nodded at the friendly receptionist as they passed by. Many were veterans, having met many times before. A few are unfamiliar, young faces.

"Good morning, guys! It's the first group of cubicles on your right," she said with a smile as she gestures in that direction.

Just around the corner, FBI Resident Agent in Charge (RAC) Mike O'Reilly greeted each officer as they entered. Mike, as always, is impeccably dressed and highly polished. He welcomes each man and woman with a warm handshake and an easy smile.

O'Reilly knew most of them from their participation in one or more of his other task forces. Even if they didn't know Mike personally, some likely recognized him from having seen him on television at one press conference or another. He always appeared as comfortable in front of a camera as any seasoned politician.

"Come in, ladies and gentlemen. Grab a seat if you can find one... In a moment, I'd like to introduce you to our new addition to the Springfield Field Office."

The well-dressed, middle-aged agent, wearing a business suit, and sporting a full head of thick, pure-white hair, stood up to face the arriving officers. He nodded and forced an uncomfortable smile.

To the officers, he appeared educated, refined, and professional. Still, not a guy they envision grabbing beers with at the local cop bar after hours. Over Rick's shoulder, some noticed a poster that he's tacked on the wall above his new desk. It was the only personal item the former "spook" hunter had in his office

The ghostly image reveals a black sky, a dark ocean, and a sinking ship. The ship is engulfed in flames and half-submerged. Its stern is concealed below the waves, as its bow remains pointing upward as if desperately reaching to escape its fate. In the foreground of the image, a single hand can be seen. It, too, desperately reaches up from the dark ocean, one last time before the victim drowns.

The caption read, "Someone Talked."

"Ladies and gentlemen, I'd like you to welcome Special Agent Rick Winfield. Rick's just arrived from our headquarters in Washington D.C. Rick's coming from our counterintelligence group."

"The spook hunters!"

One officer in the back row said with a friendly chuckle.

"Yes, you could call it that," Mike agreed with his usual easy smile.

Those in the group familiar with the spy world knew much of the Intel side of work was classified. It was all top secret and not remotely like the street work he was about to do on the new Task Force.

Many Intel agents spend entire careers exclusively doing surveillance of suspected spies. They follow them around the city from public and covert locations. That might include blending in at Embassies or high-end watering holes of D.C. The atmosphere is a world away from the places street agents go while chasing gangsters through crack houses or down the dingy alleys. Some intel agents may monitor suspected spies for years, without ever conducting an actual interview or making a single arrest.

O'Reilly continued, "As you all know, Springfield is being overrun with drugs, gangs, and gun violence. So there are plenty of bad guys needing guns to do business. But with Massachusetts having some of the strictest gun laws in America, they can't merely obtain guns through legal gun shops.

"It looks like the Russians have moved in to accommodate the demand. We think we've identified a nationwide organized crime group of Russians working right here in our city. Besides conducting their traditional businesses of extortions, robberies, trafficking in the stolen vehicles and drugs, they are cornering the market on illegal guns."

Winfield cleared his throat and then gave Mike a glance and nod. He was ready to take it from there.

Patrick Burns

"Anyway, Agent Winfield is going to lead the team," O'Reilly closed the introduction phase. "I'll let Rick get started."

As the group settled into their new working accommodations, FBI Agent Rob Lewis arrived and, without a word, grabbed a seat in the back of the room. He returns a nod, a smile, and a wave to several familiar faces in the group.

Following closely behind him was the Greek, the handlebar- mustached, crusty veteran Detective, Steve Maurangadakis from Springfield P.D. Likewise, he took a seat with just a smile and wave to the group.

Finally, a dark-skinned, thin man with one gold tooth sat down behind the two. Rob's star undercover operative, "Carlos," was there to help get the operation off to a good start.

"Thanks, Michael," Winfield said in a formal tone and a forced half-smile. Then he turned to address his new team,

"Most of you know Carlos for his work with Rob on the Gang Task Force. He's done some amazing work. Rob has graciously offered his services to our Task Force. He's going to work with us. Carlos has already infiltrated the Russian crew."

A few in the group give Carlos and Rob nods and thumbs up, showing their approval and appreciation.

Winfield flips through a collection of index card notes on his desk, "Carlos has set up our first deal. We are going to buy two AK-47s. The location is called the North End Body Shop."

"Yeah. It's also called the Russian chop shop," one of the local detectives mentions matter-of-factly.

"Right. So, as I said, Carlos is going to buy two AK 47 rifles today. Our mission is to identify the Russian players, examine the guns, and then use that information to identify their source. Once we ID the source, we can shut down the entire pipeline. Are there any questions?"

Members of the group begin to softly chat between themselves, sharing knowledge of the Russian Chop Shop and the surrounding area. A few moments later, one officer in the middle of the group raises his hand.

"I have a question. How about the ATF? Should we invite them in?"

"Thanks for the suggestion. But we don't need the ATF. This is an FBI operation."

"But gun trafficking is their specialty. They have experts, informants, and an entire gun tracing network. Wouldn't that be helpful for us?"

"The fewer people who know about our operation, the better. We'll be fine. Besides, we have Donny Brown here from Springfield P.D.," Winfield said as he gestured toward a thin, mild-mannered, and well-groomed detective seated behind the Greek. Don reacted by raising his hand and giving everyone in the group a wave and a three-finger salute from his temple.

"Don is our firearms expert. He's a certified armorer. I'm told that Don knows every gun known to man."

"But without ATF, how will we trace the guns?"

"All the guns we buy on the street from the Russians will go directly to our tech guys at the FBI lab at Quantico."

The officer who made the suggestion paused a moment and then quietly settled back in his chair. His puzzled look fell away as he glanced up at the former spook hunter's poster, "Someone Talked."

"Okay, everyone," Rick said, "if there are no more questions, let's move down the hall to our briefing room. Grab a coffee, use the head. We'll start the operational briefing in fifteen."

*****

A few miles away, the usual traffic passed by the North End Body Shop's large open garage door. From the street, several men could be seen meandering around the large hanger-style structure.

Several cars balanced atop hydraulic lifts in various stages of repair. In the back, a man in a face shield used a grinder on a metal car frame. Another man could be seen rolling a new tire along the floor. In the back room, a large, square-headed Neanderthal- looking man was on the phone.

"Yes. Yes. I'll call you as soon as the guy gets here," he replied to the Russian on the other end of the call. "Yes. Yes. OK. Yes. I know. You don't need to keep telling me. I will lead him to your store. Yes. Alex will follow behind us. If there is any sign of police, we know what to do. Right. Yes. I know. You don't have to keep telling me."

*****

On the other side of the Connecticut River, on the west side of town, the usual light traffic passed slowly along Main Street. A few pedestrians walked along the otherwise empty sidewalks. Across the street from the small strip mall that houses the Russian Book Store and AAA Gun Shop's shared parking lot, the Russian liqueur store bustled with customers. Its parking lot was full. The strip mall lot was empty except for a large trash dumpster and a couple of employee cars.

Inside AAA Guns, Big Dave and his wife tended to a customer examining a camouflage stock 30-06 rifle. In the Russian Book Store, the owner, Roman Zhirnov, a former Russian military officer, was in his private office.

Patrick Burns

He slid back a curtain to view several individuals lingering near the display area out front. He nodded as he recognized them. There were no unfamiliar faces, and everything looked safe for the deal.

Zhirnov let the curtain fall closed and returned to his desk. On it are two AK-47s. He picked the first one up and pulled back the slide. He pulled the trigger and hears the expected click. It seemed in good order. Next, he checked its markings. CAI Arms in St. Albans, VT was listed as the importer. He then looked at the section of the rifle where the serial number should be located. Zhirnov nodded to himself as he saw there was no trace of one. *Ochen' khorosho, very good,* he said as he moved to the next gun. It also checked out.

Satisfied, Zhirnov picked up the company phone and dialed a Pennsylvania number from memory. A phone rang 200 miles away in Lancaster, PA – AKA, Amish Country.

"Ello. Iz me, Roman. Yes. They are good. We will need more of the same, with no serial numbers." He paused to listen, then continued.

"Right. Don't worry. If anything goes wrong, we know what to do. We'll dump the fucker in the river."

Click. The call ended.

Zhinov put down the phone and looked out his office window into the display/sales area. It was empty.

He checked the time on his watch, looked down, and opened the desk's top drawer. Lying inside was a Russian pistol. He pulled back the slide on top, exposing one round is in the chamber. He presses the magazine ejector switch. A loaded clip popped out. He slid it back inside with a click as it snapped into place. Finally, he replaced it inside the drawer, leaving the drawer slightly open, the gun easily accessible.

*****

At the FBI office, Winfield stood at one end of a long, polished conference room table. Behind him was a whiteboard. The team listened and watched as he pointed out where each of the surveillance units would set up in the neighborhood surrounding the Russian Body Shop.

"Donny, you'll set up in position number one. Photograph anyone who comes to the street to meet Carlos. You'll be the 'eyeball.' You'll need to relay everything you see to the rest of the team.

"Carlos will park in front of the body shop. Someone will need to come out to meet him. You get a picture of anyone you see. For the deal, they'll no doubt take him inside the shop.

"Then, as soon as Carlos gives them the cash and gets the AKs, we're done. We'll then simply do security surveillance, loosely follow Carlos back to the office. And we'll make sure to never let the evidence out of an agent or officer's view.

"We'll have a good chain of custody. Once at the office, the evidence goes to Donny for inventory and identification. So, I think that's it. Rob? Do you have anything to add?"

"Thanks, Rich," Rob said. "You all know Carlos. Today he'll be driving a red Toyota. Take a look at the car. At all times, we need to have an eyeball on it. And we've wired it for sound. So if Carlos can get any of them talking in, or near it, we can record their conversation."

"Perfect!" Winfield said.

"And there's one more thing," Rob added. "It's critical that Carlos can't trip. He cannot allow them to lead him away from the body shop and into a possible trap. We only have a security perimeter on the body shop. Any other location is not protected. If the bad guys try to move the deal's location or suggest that the guns are somewhere else, Carlos will cancel the deal. We can't allow them to change the location. Going anywhere else could be an indication they are planning a rip-off."

"Thanks, Rob. I think we're ready," Rick said, returning to the head of the table to make team assignments.

Within an hour, the team set up a perimeter on the side streets surrounding the location. With everyone in place, Rick sent Carlos in.

Moments later, a red Toyota pulled up in front of a large, open garage door. Carlos parked on the street directly in front. Donny took a picture of him and then updated the surveillance teams, "CI number one is at Moscow one," Don announced on his radio.

Several men could be seen inside the bay area. Some were working on cars; others were meandering around. Donny took another photo.

Carlos scanned the street for any suspicious-looking characters or signs of a rip-off. Nothing struck him as a red flag of danger. It looked like a 'go.'

"I'm here, at the place," he said, holding his cell phone to one ear and pretending to make a phone call knowing the microphones in the dashboard of his car were relaying his message. "I'm going in."

"Stand by, everyone; our guy is going inside," Donny said as he snapped off a picture of the CI stepping out of his car and walking into the garage toward the unidentified Russians inside.

Officer Brown watched as Carlos spoke to two men inside the garage area. Brown couldn't hear the conversation; only the car was wired for sound.

Patrick Burns

“All units, he's talking to a couple of workers inside the garage. Stand by."

“What's going on, Donny?" Winfield asked. "Where is he?”

“Stand by. I think I see him coming now.”

“Does he have the guns?” Winfield asked.

“Negative. He's getting back into his car. And it looks like the two guys from the garage are getting into a black Lexus parked on the street. Stand by.”

"Rob. You told him there'd be no tripping, right? This could be a rip-off!"

"Yep, I did. But Carlos doesn't always go by the book. And he's got brass balls. If he leaves, we need to just keep up."

“CI One is leaving," Donny reported. "He's headed South on Acorn Street. The black Lexis is right behind him. One male driver and one passenger.”

“Shit! Everyone, CI is Tripping! CI is Tripping! Follow the red Toyota. Targets are in a black Lexis.”

“This is Tango four. I'm still watching the body shop. It looks like a second car is trying to catch up with the CI and the Lexis.”

"Should we pull him out, Rich? This could be a rip?"

"Hold on, everyone. This is Rob. Give him a little more time. But keep an eye on him. We have the car wired. He'll call for help if he smells trouble."

Minutes later, the caravan of cars crested the Memorial Bridge, crossing the Connecticut River on their way to the west side, the Russian side of town.

Carlos sensed that the agents were on edge and might be considering moving in and ending the deal. He continued to drive, pretending to sing to the music on the radio.

"Guys, yo, I got it covered. We're going to the west side. I'm turning onto Main Street, coming up to the Russian Book Store and AAA Guns shop.

"Everyone!" Donny advised the teams. "He's on Main Street, west side. Work your way into the area."

Officers and agents feared the worst. This was becoming a perfect scenario for Carlos to be robbed and killed.

"Guys, "Officer Brown said, "I've got the eyeball. I'm two cars behind him, coming up to the bookstore. OK. Now we're passing the bookstore, now we're at AAA Guns. Stand by."

"What are they doing?" Winfield asked.

Patrick Burns

"Looks like his left directional is on. They're going to turn left into the plaza where the gun shop and bookstore are."

"That's a dead end," one team member, familiar with the location, said on the radio.

"Officer Brown, DO NOT FOLLOW him onto that street!" Winfield shouted. "It's a dead end. There is no way out of there, and you'll be spotted. Set up best you can with a vantage point of that side street, but don't get any closer."

The team members scrambled to set up at locations with a clear view of the parking lot behind the bookstore and gun shop.

But it was impossible.

"They're in the alley behind the gun shop and bookstore," Brown said. "Our guy is going inside with the two Russians. He's taking the bag with buy money inside."

"Going inside which business?" Winfield asked.

"I can't tell from here. There are a couple of doors in the back. One looks like it goes to the gun store and the other to the bookstore. It looks like he went into the first or second door, but I can't tell for sure from this angle."

"Shit! We don't even know where he is now!" said one officer. "They could be killing him right now!"

"Should we move in?" another officer asks.

"Everyone, calm down," Rob said. "Give him a few minutes."

Seconds seem like hours as time passes. Everyone is ready to bust down the door to rescue the CI.

And then, finally, "They're coming out," Brown said, "Stand by."

Brown raises his camera and snaps a picture. As he twists the lens to focus, a blurry image consumed the entire lens. He lowered the camera. A gray-haired man with a cane left the liquor store and stood in front of Don's car. The man looked directly at Carlos and the Russians as they loaded the guns into the car trunk.

"Stand by," Donny said quickly. "We have a civilian here."

The elderly man turned and continued walking toward the sidewalk. Carlos finished loading two AK 47s into the trunk of his car. Donny raised his camera for another photo, but the Russians had turned their backs, walking toward the door. He snapped a picture just as they close the door.

"Shit!"

Patrick Burns

"Everyone," Winfield commands. "The red Toyota is on Main Street and heading east. Follow it back to the office. Let's go!"

Seconds later, the undercover car and surveillance teams disappeared into the Main Street traffic.

The red Toyota and security caravan wound their way through the west side and then over the Memorial Bridge, on the way back to the FBI office on the other side of town. Meanwhile, inside the bookstore, the shop owner picked up his desk phone and dialed. A cell phone rang hundreds of miles away, inside a dilapidated farmer's barn surrounded by cornfields.

"Ello?"

"Ivan. It's me, Roman."

"Well?"

"It's done. We got $1,800 for both."

"No problems?"

"No. It all went good, and the guy wants more."

"Very nice work, my friend. We can get as many as you need."

12   *The Straw Purchase*

The next day, it was a typical morning at the ATF office. Since I was not part of the FBI Task Force, I was unaware of their deal at the Russian Book Store. So, as usual, I grabbed a handful of messages from the fax machine, grabbed a coffee, and switched on my computer to process gun trace requests.

By mid-morning, I'd finished the last of them. Soon the technicians in West Virginia would make phone calls to various gun dealers and manufacturers throughout the country. On my way to grabbing another coffee in the next room, the office phone rang.

"Hello. ATF?" I answered.

From the parking lot pay phone at the West Side Liquor Store, a gray-haired man leaning on a wooden cane replied on the other end.

"I want to report someone selling guns. In broad daylight, they sell them right out of the trunk of a car!"

"Where?"

"In a parking lot behind the West Side Book Store," the elderly caller reported.

"Who is this I'm speaking with?"

Patrick Burns

"I don't want to identify myself. I don't want to get involved. But listen. I'm looking at one of the cars right now. The same cars are here again today. There's no one that I see. But the same cars are here again. You should come to investigate."

"I can meet you over there right now. Just give me a few minutes."

"No. Like I said, I don't want to get involved. I don't want to be identified or killed. No thanks. I'm a veteran. I just want to report what I saw. They were military weapons. There were rifles, maybe even grenade launchers. I can't say for sure. But they were loading guns into a car trunk."

"Okay. So how did you see this?"

"I was buying my gin as I do each week. This store has the best prices on my gin. I'm a veteran like I said. Anyway, when I was leaving the liquor store, I saw them. I was walking by. That's all. You need to look into it! I did my part!"

Click, the line went dead.

"Hello?"

*****

Within minutes, I was racing to the scene. I pulled into the parking lot behind the bookstore and took out my notepad to jot down all the license plate numbers of cars parked nearby. Then I grabbed my car radio transmitter.

"Hello, this is the Springfield office calling Boston. Can someone run two plates for me?"

"This is Boston. Go ahead, Pat."

"Two plates as follows: Massachusetts Zebra Echo 8765, ZE 8765, and Alfa November 4532, AN 4532, over."

"Stand by Pat," the Boston agent says as she queries the database. "The first comes back to a Roman Zhirnov, and the Honda comes back to an Aleksei Safanov. Both have addresses in West Springfield, Massachusetts. Over."

"Thank you, Boston. I'll check criminal history myself when I get back. Over. Thanks again."

"10-4, Pat. You're welcome. Good luck!"

I killed the engine, hopped out of the car, and walked around to the front of the shops. A moment later, a cowbell rang as I entered the front door of AAA Guns.

Dave looked up from behind the long glass showcase. As always, it was filled with assorted weapons. His white-haired wife was tending the books, as always, in her folding chair behind him.

Patrick Burns

"Dave, do you know anything about the guys in the business next door?"

"Only that they're assholes."

"What do you mean?"

"They dump their trash on my back step. But that's about all I know about 'em."

"What about guns? Did you sell any guns to them?"

"No, they don't come in here. But watch out when you deal with those guys. Those Russians are some cold-blooded bastards. I think they'd kill you as soon as look at you."

"Thanks, Dave. No problem."

*****

Still parked behind the Russian Book Store, where the deal had recently gone down, I took another moment before I started the car. I dialed my cell phone.

"Hello, FBI. Springfield. How may I help you?"

"Hi Karen, it's Pat Burns from ATF. Are any of the agents from the Russian Task Force in?"

"Yes, sure. Hold on."

The receptionist walks down the hall to the conference room at the end of the building. Inside, laid out on the long, polished wooden table, there are two disassembled AK-47s. Donny is seated next to them, eyeglasses dangling on the tip of his nose, a set of tools in-hand. Agent Winfield and other Task Force members looked on.

"Nope. Rick, there's nothing," Donny says to Winfield and the others. "There are no serial numbers on either gun. I can't even find a place where it looks like they've been removed. It seems like they never *had* serial numbers in the first place."

"Interesting," Winfield said. "Do you think the gun importer is in on this? Maybe the guns were smuggled into the country?"

"Anything's possible. But if there ever *were* serial numbers, the removal was absolutely perfect. It's the most professional job I've ever seen."

Just then, the conference room door slowly swung open. The receptionist was standing in the threshold, leaning into the room.

"Sorry to interrupt, Rick. But there's an ATF agent on the phone. He wants to speak with someone about the Russians."

"Thank you, Karen," Rick replied dismissively as he rolled his eyes. "Tell him we'll call him back."

As Karen disappeared around the corner back to her desk, Rick turned to one of the other Springfield officers

182

seated at the conference table. "Tom, why don't you take the call. See what this guy wants."

As Sheehan dialed my office, Donny moved on to examining the remaining evidence. He began spreading out the pictures taken during the undercover gun buy.

Tom Sheehan returned. "Rick. He wants to join the Task Force. He says he has information on the Russians."

Rick looks over and simply shakes his head, "No."

Sheehan got back to me. "Sorry, Pat. He says the team is full right now."

"Okay. Well, I have some information about the Russians trafficking guns, so I already opened a case. At this point, I can't just ignore it. I have no choice but to investigate, one way or the other, on your team or alone."

"I understand, Pat," Sheehan said apologetically.

"Okay, then. Thanks, Tom."

The phone call ended just as Donny finished spreading out the last of the photos.

"Shit!" he complained.

The pictures were from a long distance and blurry. Some are photos of people's backs and closed doors.

"The photos are no good," Donny said. "Sorry, Rick. We can't use these for a positive ID on any of these guys."

"Well, folks," Winfield said. "We have two guns, with no serial numbers. And we have two dozen photographs not usable in court. Looks like it's back to the drawing board. We need another deal. Let Rob know. Ask him if Carlos is available."

*****

A few days later, standing inside the farmer's barn in Amish Country, a short Russian dials his cell phone.

Another phone rings in the next town over.

A thin, pasty-skinned man with a mosaic of multicolored teeth—deep yellows and browns—sits in a folding chair in the kitchen of his ramshackle apartment. As the phone rings for the third time, he slides a straw up into his nose as he leans forward. His face is now inches away from a hand mirror; he aims the other end of the straw toward a thin line of white powder.

Snorting the line of coke, he sits up abruptly, taking a nose full of air, forcing the cocaine in further. As he does, he grabs the ringing phone. "Yeah?"

Patrick Burns

"It's me. Get your skinny ass out of bed. We have work to do. Don't be late again," Teleguz snaps the phone closed. "Fuckin' junkie!"

*****

Forty minutes later, the emaciated man pulled his junker of a car into a parking lot behind Bob's Sporting Goods store, killing the engine. After knocking and belching smoke for a moment, the engine settled down and went quiet.

As the thin man rolled down his window, his nervous, sunken eyes darted back and forth. He took repeated puffs off of a cigarette, trying to take the edge off, but instead just filled the car with smoke.

Moments later, he breathed a sigh of relief as he saw a green pickup truck pulling into the lot. A rough-looking Russian pulled up next to the thin man's junker.

"Here," Teleguz said, handing the man a wad of cash. "You go in first. I'll follow you and point out which guns to buy."

Inside the store, the emaciated man spotted Bob, the shop owner, standing behind one showcase. He took a deep breath to calm his withdrawal shakes, offering a nervous smile to the owner, exposing his collection of rotten teeth.

The shop owner said nothing, just smiled and nods, well accustomed to the fact that his customers come in all shapes and sizes.

Both men perused the gun showcases separately. They purposely avoided speaking to each other, except in sporadic whispers.

Finally, Teleguz gave his accomplice a nod. He gestured toward a used .40 caliber pistol inside the display case. A few moments later, he walked further down the aisle and spotted a .25 caliber pistol. The thin man called for the shop owner to assist.

"I'd like these two pistols, sir," the thin man said with a patronizing smile, again exposing his yellow teeth.

Teleguz meanders around in the background, pretending to still be considering buying one himself.

"Do you have an ID?" the shop owner asked the buyer.

The man handed him a driver's license. The shop owner reached under the counter for the required paperwork, a bill of sale, a receipt, and an ATF Form 4473. The law requires it to be completed by each purchaser for each firearm. It also requires that the form be signed under oath.

Patrick Burns

The buyer checked off the boxes on the form and filled in his answers in the appropriate spaces. He listed all the information, name, address, and so on. Eventually, he got to the most critical question. *Are you buying the listed firearm for yourself?*

He checked the box, *Yes.*

Claiming to buy a firearm for oneself while knowing it is actually for another person is called a Straw Purchase. The penalty for the false answer on the ATF form is up to five years in federal prison for each falsely signed form. He bought two guns. He's facing ten years if caught.

But the drive of cocaine addiction trumps the risk.

Moments later, with the two guns inside a shopping bag, Quickel gave Bob another shaky, patronizing smile. Beads of sweat slid down his temples as he headed to the door. Relief was just around the corner; he'll get paid and can buy more blow.

Hurrying around the building's outside corner, he saw Teleguz waiting with his payment for the deal.

The Russian said nothing. He gave the thin man an impatient look, a $100 bill, grabbed the guns, and, seconds later, hopped back into his truck. Teleguz fired up the engine, pulled onto the highway, and headed back to the farmhouse.

Thirty minutes later, Teleguz delivered the guns to his crew. They disassembled the firearms to expose the parts with serial numbers. Next, the worker put on a set of thick gloves and a welder's mask. The gun parts are laid out onto the rickety wooden workbench. Teleguz stood in the background watching as the men used a hand-held grinding machine.

The tool hums as the worker gradually applied the spinning wheel to where the serial numbers are etched on the first gun's barrel. As he does, the ear-grating screech of metal on metal echoed off the walls. Bright sparks fly into the darkened barn's rafters, like fireworks sparklers on the Fourth of July.

Without a word, the worker finishes grinding, re-bluing, and then re-assembling each gun. In little time, each weapon looks as if the serial numbers never existed. Teleguz dials his cell phone. A second later, a phone rings 200 miles away on the West Side of Springfield. Inside the Russian Book Store's backroom, the former Russian military officer, Roman Zhirnov, answers.

"Ello?"

"It's me. Your order is ready!"

The next morning, a few miles away, I'm back inside the ATF office on the other side of the Connecticut River. As I reviewed gun reports, a small, black and white television is on in the next room. I can't see it, but I can hear it.

"Breaking news! A commercial plane has just hit the World Trade Center!"

I rush into the next room and watch the video. Amazingly, a second plane hits the second tower. Both Twin Towers are engulfed in smoke and flames. Soon afterward, additional reports—an attack on the Pentagon and a fourth plane crashing in a rural field—come across the screen.

It is September 11, 2001.

As of that very moment, the FBI re-tasked every agent in America to working terrorism cases. That order included those who had been assigned to the Russian Task Force. The AK-47s purchased at the Russian Book Store were now at the lab at Quantico. They remained there, in a vault, stored indefinitely until further notice.

I'm also assigned to work on the FBI's Terrorism Task Force, while my Russian investigation is also put on hold.

*****

By 2002, as America recovers from the 9/11 attacks and everyone's terrorism fears ease, Springfield's Russian investigations come back to life.

On June 24, 2002, Carlos and the Tasks Force buy four firearms from the Russians. None have serial numbers. On July 16, 2002, the team bought five more guns. On August 25, 2002, they purchased another eight guns. The evidence vault fills with Russian weapons.

But, despite all diligent attempts, the Quantico lab technicians cannot raise the obliterated serial numbers. Therefore, tracing the guns through the traditional system, in ATF's Gun Trace Center, is impossible.

But there might be another way to find the source of the guns. I know, from my other gun trafficking investigations, there's always been a frontman—one person, a non-felon, who buys the firearms directly from gun dealers.

A perfect example of that was my investigation of Raphael Perez. It had begun with a suspiciously extensive list of guns. From that list, I followed the trail that led to the criminals.

Somewhere out there, I know there's a gun shop with sales records that match the list of guns sitting in the FBI vault.

Even without serial numbers, I would eventually follow it to locate my gun trafficker if I could find that matching list.

But I'd already inquired at the only gun shop on the west side, the Russian side of town. The Russians bought no guns there. So without a national database to search, the only way to find that specific list of firearms and who bought them would be to find the right gun store. And locating that store, of all the gun stores in America, would be like finding a needle in a haystack. It wouldn't be impossible, but it would require a lucky break.

13   *A Lucky Break*

By 2004 the Russian weapons are still collecting dust at the FBI's vault at Quantico. The evidence waiting for someone to match it to the source, the gun trafficker who supplied them all to the Russians.

Likewise, three years have passed in the now cold-case murder investigation of Stephanie Sipe. Investigators Guth and Whitfield remain stymied. The DNA evidence still waited for someone to match it to a suspect.

The first break arrived on one dark night, on a tree-lined street on the west side of town. It was almost midnight when the local police department received a call.

"911, what's the nature of your emergency?" asked the call center operator.

On the other end of the call, a terrified man, holding a cell phone to his ear while slowly holding back the curtain, looks to see if the car is still parked at the curb in front of his house.

"He's going to kill me!" he yelled to the 911 operator.

"Who is going to kill you?"

Patrick Burns

"He's parked in front of my house. He's in a black Honda. Send someone. NOW!"

"Sir, calm down. Why do you think someone is going to kill you?"

"He's got a gun, an assault rifle. He put it up to my head two minutes ago. He told me he will kill me if I don't pay him."

"Is he still there now?"

"Yes! Yes! I slammed the door, and he went back to his car. But he's still out there. Please, HURRY!"

The man looks again. The driver is still out there, sitting alone in the car, smoking a cigarette, and watching him. The driver intentionally makes eye contact with the frightened man peeking out the window. The Russian driver smiles and points his finger at him, shaping his hand like a gun.

The frightened caller drops the curtain and pushes the living room furniture up against the door. Seconds later, he peeks out the front window again.

Suddenly the dark street is lit with flashing red and blue lights. A bright spotlight illuminates the Honda. The driver is visible inside the front seat as a police car rolls up behind him.

The officer slowly steps out of his vehicle, draws his weapon, and approaches the car from the driver's side.

As he cautiously approaches the Honda's rear door, he aims his flashlight into the back seat, looking to make sure no one else is hiding there. That's when he spots it—the barrel of an AK-47.

Immediately, the officer takes one step backward and changes his stance. He's now on high alert.

"Hands up! You, inside the car! Hands up!" He points his gun at the driver's head.

The driver casually raises one hand. He pauses and then takes a puff off his cigarette using his other hand. As he does this, he looks over toward the house again, making eye contact with the victim. The message is clear: I know you called the cops. You will pay for this.

As the spotlight lights up the driver's face, his calm, emotionless features become visible. There is no sign of panic in his dark, cold eyes, not even any sign of concern. It's more like he's annoyed by this minor inconvenience.

"Driver, with your hands up, step out of the car!" the officer yells again.

More flashing lights suddenly illuminate the rest of the street as a second police cruiser arrives on the scene. It screeches to a halt and blocks the other side of the road. A second officer leaps from his car, drawing his weapon as he does, and then he rushes in.

Patrick Burns

The officers seize the AK-47, then handcuff the suspect. One cop removes the suspect's wallet and looks for his driver's license.

"Sir, you are being arrested for threatening with a deadly weapon," one officer said. "You have the right to remain silent."

"Threatening who? You have no witness," the driver says with a heavy Russian accent. "You Americans are all cowards. Do you think that the coward who is hiding behind the curtained window will show up to court? I promise you. He won't!" he smiles, then spits on the street.

"And you are being charged with possessing an unregistered firearm," the other officer added after running the suspect's name through the state firearms records database and finding no record.

"Fuck that! Do you think I'm afraid to pay a $500 fine or spend a weekend in your cushy jails? I'm from Russia. You are all idiots! You are wasting your time!"

"We'll see about that, tough guy," one officer says as they throw him into the back seat of the first cruiser. The second officer takes custody of the rifle and waits for the tow truck to arrive for the car.

*****

The next morning, sitting alone in the ATF office, sipping on a Dunkin Donuts coffee, I read through the previous day's incoming crime-gun reports. I come across an arrest report with a familiar name, Aleksei Safanov!

This is the lucky break I needed. The report says Safanov was caught with a firearm while committing a crime of violence. Not only that, the gun had no serial numbers. Possession of a firearm without a serial number carried a sentence of 10 years.

I researched his criminal background; Safanov had a prior conviction. It's illegal for a felon to have a firearm. The penalty for that was another five years in federal prison.

Safanov didn't know it yet, but his state problems were minor compared to his ATF charges. He was now looking at fifteen years in a federal penitentiary without the possibility of parole. I typed up an arrest warrant. I'd submit it to a federal judge at the right moment.

For now, my next call was to the Massachusetts Forensics Laboratory. Safanov's AK-47 was shipped there. Unlike all the other weapons sent to the FBI. Lab, Safanov's AK-47 went to the Massachusetts State Police lab.

For me, that was lucky break number two.

It was a one-hour drive east toward Boston. After exiting Route 90, I traveled along a service road for another quarter-hour before reaching a single-story brick building at the end of a single lane road and surrounded by a heavily wooded area.

Inside the building, there were technicians in one room. They were firing guns seized from crimes into cans filled with sand. After firing, the slugs were retrieved from the sand and put under microscopes. The technicians would then inspect the grooves along their sides. Then, the groove patterns' images were compared to the grove patterns of the slugs removed from the victim's body.

In the next room, I found Sergeant Murphy. On a stainless-steel table in front of him, below a large magnifying glass, was an AK-47. Many of its parts had been removed and were lying next to the barrel and stock.

"Well? Any luck?" I asked.

"Well, I looked in all the usual locations, first on the barrel, of course, then on the bolt, the bolt carrier, then the receiver cover. And there was nothing left. All the serial numbers were completely gone."

"So that's it? We're at a dead end?"

"I thought so. But then I remembered that some of the Romanian models have serial numbers concealed under the plate above the trigger guard."

"And?"

Murphy pointed to a section on the gun frame where I could see the blue color removed by the investigator trying to recover the serial number.

"The serial was right here. It was ground off pretty good. I worked on it for a solid hour.

"And?"

"I was able to get you five digits," he said while handing me a report. Sergeant Murphy recovered the numbers 91670."

"But there should be more digits than that in the serial number, right?"

"Yes. There should be eleven numbers in the complete serial number. But I could only recover five out of the eleven digits. Sorry about that. I went down as far as I could go. Any further grinding, I'd have gone all the way through the frame. I couldn't get more. That's the best we can do, five digits."

"Okay. Thanks very much. You've been a big help."

Disappointed, I took the long drive back to the office. My lucky break had become a bust. There is no way I could trace this gun without a complete serial number.

*****

An hour later, back at the ATF office, I dial the telephone number for CAI / Century Arms of Vermont.

Patrick Burns

Aside from the five digits remaining of the serial number, the importer's name and location were all that remained on the weapon.

Without a full serial number, I knew it would be all but impossible for them to tell me where they shipped that gun. But I had to at least make the call.

"Hello, this is Patrick Burns. I'm a Special Agent with the ATF. I'm trying to trace an AK-47 you imported.

"Please hold," said the receptionist.

A moment later, the call was redirected to the accounting/shipping department.

"Hello, Bill Bradley speaking," a man's voice came onto the phone line.

"Hi, Bill. This is Pat Burns from the ATF. I'm trying to trace an AK-47 that you imported."

"Sure, no problem. Go ahead. What's the serial number?"

"It has the following numbers in this sequence, 91670," I said and paused a moment.

"Go ahead. I'm listening. What's the rest of it? There are eleven digits to the serial number on that weapon, not five."

"The thing is, I don't have the other numbers. They were ground off. We could only recover the five digits."

Bradley chuckled on the other end. "Well, agent, I hate to be the bearer of bad news, but we import thousands of those AK-47s each year. We sell them all over the country. With only five digits, it's impossible to trace. We'd have no idea where that gun was shipped to."

"The five digits are in that exact sequence," I added, urging him to look anyway.

"I can try. But I don't hold out much hope," Bradley continued, trying to convince me to accept that it was impossible.

"Listen, Bill, I don't care how many AK-47s you sold. I don't care if you sold 1,000 with numbers in that sequence. I want you to give me a listing of every single AK-47 that you sold that had those exact digits in that exact sequence. Let me worry about the next step."

"Okay. We can do that and get back to you. I don't know how long it could take."

"Not a problem. Thanks, Bill. If needed, I'll contact the destination of every single one of them. Sooner or later, by the process of elimination, I'll find out who bought that gun. So, just get me the list!"

Patrick Burns

"Barbara," Bradley told his assistant, "we need to prepare a list of all of the AK-47's we sold with these five digits in their serial numbers in this exact sequence."

She looked up at him, speechless for a moment, and then asked, "That could be thousands of guns. Do you want them all?"

"Yes, please. It's for the ATF. Big case, I guess. Please give the list to me in the morning. Have a good night."

As the door closed behind the boss, she picked up the note with the five digits written on it. She checked her watch and sighed, hoping this would not take all night. But just moments later, as the screen lit up with the displayed result, she was pleasantly surprised.

*****

The next morning, bright and early, I receive a call from Bill Bradley at CAI. Arms.

"Agent Burns?"

"Yes? Did you find anything? Do you have the list? Can you fax it to me?"

"You won't need it. Do you have a pen and pad?"

"What do you mean?"

"You must have the luck of the Irish," Bradley said with a chuckle.

"What are you saying?"

"There's only one gun! We only sold one AK-47 with precisely those five digits in that exact sequence! Therefore, we've identified the rifle in our sales records. And since there is only one AK-47 with that sequence of digits, I can tell you what the other six digits were!"

"Amazing! I can't believe it!"

"And that's not all, not only can I tell you the complete serial number, but I can also tell you the date that we sold it as well as the name of the gun store we sold it to, their address, and the date we shipped it."

I don't know how to measure smiles, but I must have had one of the biggest ever.

14   *Can I Tell the Truth <u>NOW</u>?*

The following day, I typed the AK-47's complete eleven digits serial number into our database. I entered it into the file for the Russians. In the summer of 2001, the rifle had been shipped to Jimmy's Sporting Goods in Fairhope, Alabama.

"Hello! Jimmy's Sporting Goods!"

After a conversation with Jimmy, he sent me a shipping record. Savonov's AK-47 was received with a second AK-47 from Century Arms. One rifle was sold to a customer; Safanov's AK-47 was sold to another gun shop. Jimmy gave me the name and address of that gun shop. In 2001, it was shipped to Bob's Sporting Goods in Lancaster, Pennsylvania, Amish Country.

"Hello? ATF Philadelphia, may I help you?"

"Hello, ATF Philadelphia. It's Pat Burns with ATF Springfield. I need someone to pay a visit to one of your local gun shops for me..."

"No problem. I'll connect you with Agent Jim Watson. Just a moment, please."

The following day, bright and early, ATF Special Agent Jim Watson arrived at Bob's Sporting Goods in Lancaster.

After displaying his badge and introducing himself, Watson informed Bob he was conducting a routine record inspection.

"Any particular person you're interested in? Would you like me to look for a particular gun sale agent?"

"Thanks, Bob. But I'd like to handle it myself and look over your sales. I don't have a target name to offer. It's just routine."

Agent Watson took the gun transaction journal to a nearby countertop. As Bob tended to customers, Jim flipped the pages for the summer of 2001, the time frame immediately after Safanov's gun shipped from Jimmy's Sporting Goods in Fairhope, Alabama.

A few moments later, one entry caught his eye. Listed on the *Received From* line is an AK-47 from Jimmy's. Perfect. Watson follows the line on the page across to the next heading, *Serial Number.* Watson looks over his shoulder at Bob, still busy with customers.

Watson removed a slip of paper with the serial number of Safanov's AK-47, comparing it to the gun shop record. Bingo! It's a match. Following the line on the page to the heading, *Purchaser.* A Michael Quickel purchased the gun. Bingo again! He had found the straw purchaser!

Watson asked Bob to review the ATF forms on file. Request granted. Photocopying all the documents filed for Michael Quickel, he added them to his case file. As he finished, Watson knew that stopping at a single gun shop is like trying one potato chip to a straw purchaser. You can't just have one. To conceal their activities and stay below the government radar, traffickers often use multiple gun shops for their acquisitions.

Agent Watson thanked the shop owner and left. He hopped into his G-ride. Next stop, Harry's Bait and Tackle.

Watson will spend the entire day making 'routine book inspections' at all other local gun shops. But these searches won't be focused on an AK-47 or a particular time frame. These records searches will be for all purchases by Michael Quickel.

Agent Watson arrived back at the Philadelphia ATF office. He tossed a stack of ATF forms 4473 onto his desk and then picked up the telephone.

"Pat. I think I found what you were looking for!"

I compared his results to my list of guns put onto the street by the Russians in Springfield; every make, model, caliber, and barrel length, is a perfect match!

*****

By noon the next day, I hit the road. I headed up the ramp toward Route 95 South with a bag lunch and a drink toward Pennsylvania. Six hours later, as the sun sets at dinner time, I pulled into the parking lot for the Applebee's in Lancaster.

Sitting alone at a corner table, I spot an impeccably groomed, well-dressed State Trooper, Corporal Ray Guth, Pennsylvania State Police. He's in plain clothes, wearing crisply starched blue jeans with a razor-sharp crease, a white cowboy hat, and spit-polished boots.

"Corporal Guth, I presume?"

He nods, and I take a seat. After the waitress takes our order, we discuss our strategy for approaching Quickel, our target. Guth also has another target in mind. So this effort will catch two birds with one stone.

"First off, you should know that I don't have enough evidence to search Quickel's apartment or to arrest him," I explained to Ray. We were quickly on a first-name basis.

"Okay," Ray nodded.

"What I do have is an address for him. It's listed on the forms he filed to buy the guns. But it's dated 2001. It's been three years. So I don't know if he's even going to be in the same place."

"He's not," Guth replies and then hands me a computer printout. It lists an address Quickel had more recently used, April of this year. That is when he renewed his driver's license.

Patrick Burns

"Okay, so if he's still at this address, at least we can find him, maybe. Next issue, he has the right to remain silent. So I can't force him to talk to us."

"Yes. I know," Guth said as our burgers arrived.

"If we do find he's still living at this new address—a big *if*—and if he's home tonight—another *if*— and if he is fool enough to answer the door—yet another *if*—we still need to talk our way inside."

"Right."

"He needs to invite us inside voluntarily."

"Agreed."

"To get inside, we need him to let his guard down. We'll have a zero percent chance to get inside if I start by telling him he's my target. If I say that, I think he'll simply demand a lawyer and then slam the door in our faces.

"If he does that, I'm done.

"I'll drive six hours back to Massachusetts empty-handed. And tomorrow, his lawyer will likely advise him to file a belated theft report for those guns. At that point, it will be all over. It will be impossible to disprove his cover story. There's no way I could prove the guns weren't stolen from his possession."

"I'm with you. Got it."

"So, I think, if he opens the door tonight, I'll offer a friendly smile and introduce us while putting him to ease. I'll inform him that one of my responsibilities is to make sure gun shops file all the required gun sales forms. I'll tell him I was hoping he could help me by reviewing a few reports filed by Bob's Sporting Goods."

"Okay. If you say so."

"Once he thinks we are on the wrong trail, he may be inclined to let us in. And if we do get in, I plan to give him as much rope as he needs to hang himself."

"What do you mean?"

"Just follow my lead. You'll see."

The waitress places the bill on the table. Guth reaches to grab it. I beat him to it. "I've got this, Ray. Without your help, I'd be lost down here, deep in farmland USA."

Moments later, we were on our way to meet Quickel.

*****

Corporal Guth and I arrive at a dimly lit apartment complex. Half of the parking lot lamps are burnt out. The cars are mixed; some late models, others are not.

"That's his unit," Guth says after comparing the number on the door to his license information.

Patrick Burns

"Here we go."

As we walked up to the front door, the room next to the door is our suspect's. A thin curtain blocked a clear view, but silhouettes can be seen meandering inside.

Standing on the front step, I knocked on the door and waited for a moment. I looked over at Ray. He nodded.

We heard faint sounds coming from the other side of the door. It sounds like whispering and moving of furniture. Changing positions—from standing in front of the entrance to standing on either of it—I move to the left and Ray to the right.

We both know it wouldn't be the first time officers were ambushed like this.

We waited.

I knocked again. We waited.

Finally, we heard a metal chain sliding against the lock. The door opened slightly.

Standing in the gap of the half-opened door, the bare-chested, emaciated-looking young man with pasty white skin smiles, exposing a train wreck of teeth.

"Yes?"

"Michael Quickel?" I ask, purposely not yet identifying myself. Guth and I are both dressed in casual clothes with badges and guns concealed.

"Who are you?" he asks with a blank look and fading smile.

"I'm with the ATF," I raise my badge for his inspection. Guth does the same. "I was hoping you could help us."

"Me? Help you?"

"Yes. One of my jobs is to make sure gun dealers file the proper reports of their sales. I have a couple of reports filed by Bob's Sporting Goods. I'd like you to review them and confirm if Bob filled them out properly. I believe you may have purchased a couple of guns there?"

Quickel nods, sensing no danger. "Sure," he says while opening the door and inviting us inside.

Guth and I share a nod. This is working out better than we expected. We followed Quickel inside the ramshackle apartment. He led us to his kitchen, inviting us to take seats at the table.

So far, so good.

"Here are the forms. By the way, thanks for the help." I placed three gun purchase forms on the table.

Patrick Burns

The remaining dozen forms I kept out of sight for the time being. At the right moment, they will also appear.

Quickel leaned down toward the table and inspected each of the ATF form 4473s, forms he completed and signed under penalty of perjury.

"Did you buy those guns?" I asked him. "Did Bob fill out the forms properly? Is that your signature on each?"

"Yep. They look right. That's my signature."

"Great!"

Quickel sat back in the kitchen chair as Guth says nothing. He simply watches with a poker face. He also has questions of his own that he plans to ask at the right moment.

I continue. "I have a few forms here that were filed by Tom's Guns and Hunting Supplies and a couple of other places. Can you look at them also and tell me if they reflect actual gun sales? They seem to have you listed as the purchaser," I said as I passed more ATF form 4473s across the kitchen table to him.

The thin, pasty man looks them all over. He seems optimistic, content with how smoothly he's handling us. Finally, he inspects the final form and looks up to us. He nods.

"Yes," he says with a smile. "These are accurate, too."

"Great. And are those your signatures on all of the forms?"

"Yep. That's my signature."

He's unaware that one of the forms is for the AK-47 with an obliterated serial number that turned up on the street in Springfield more than a year ago.

"Great!" I look over to Guth. He's chomping at the bit. But we have to do this step by step.

"Can I ask you if you purchased any other firearms?"

"Yes. Over the years, I bought more than a dozen. I like guns."

"I understand. There's nothing wrong with buying guns. By the way, it sounds like you have quite a collection. Officer Guth is a collector also. May we see them?"

Guth and I both know this would be impossible. All the guns he purchased have been sitting in the FBI vault in Virginia for more than a year.

Quickel sat back in his chair—fidgeting and stuttering—as he searches for an explanation. "Well, I don't keep them here."

Patrick Burns

I give Guth a look. We both know this is Quickel's first big mistake, besides his error of letting us in the door.

"Oh, really? So, where are they being kept?"

"I keep them at a friend's house. More secure."

"Ah. I see." I glance again at Guth, thinking, this is where we give Quickel all the rope he needs to hang himself.

"What's the friend's name?"

"I'd rather not get him involved."

Guth and I pretend not to be suspicious. "Okay. Does he live nearby? A place where you can access your guns if you need them?"

"He lives on a road near cornfields. It's not far from here. There's a dinosaur on the end of his street."

Guth's eyes widened when he heard that location. The 'friend' lives near the landmark dinosaur. He knows precisely who lived on that street—the Russian who killed Stephanie Sipe. Without a word, he reached inside his notebook file to confirm he had a photo array of his suspect. He kept it out of sight for now and waited for the right moment.

"Okay," I replied as I pull out an affidavit form. "I appreciate the help. I need to get it all down, so I don't forget. I'll let you use your own words, review the form, and sign it when we're done. Sound good?"

Quickel smiled and nodded. As far as he knows, this is all going along just fine.

"So, where was I?" ...

I ask as I jot down each question and his answers. "Oh, by the way, why aren't the guns being kept here at your apartment?"

"My apartment is tiny. It's only got one bedroom. There's not enough room to keep them here."

"Oh. I see. Yes. It is small here. By the way, when did you move here?" I ask, as Guth peeks down at the car registration note that said Quickel moved to this address in April of this year.

"I moved here in April."

"April of this year?"

"Yes."

"So you purchased thirteen guns, including the guns referred to on the signed 4473 forms that I have shown you today. Is that correct?"

"Yes. That's correct."

Patrick Burns

"And all of the guns were moved to your friend's house in April of this year because you didn't have enough room in this new apartment?"

"Yes. That's right."

"And you moved here when?"

"April this year."

"So you personally moved the guns? You and your friend?"

"Yes."

"Did you use your car or his car?"

"We used his car."

"What type of car did you use?"

"He has a pickup truck."

"What color is his truck?"

"Green."

Corporal Guth nodded and grins. He knows exactly which truck Quickel is referring to.

I continued writing his statements onto the affidavit form, knowing it's all lies but allowing him to talk his way into a corner he can't escape from.

"So, in April, you and your friend carried all of the guns from this apartment to his house?"

"Correct."

"You personally loaded them into his truck?"

"Yes."

"You personally drove to his house with him and then unloaded all of the guns into his house?"

"Yes."

"Which room at his house did you load the guns into after you removed them from his green pickup truck in April of this year?"

"We put them in his living room."

"Great! I think we have what we need," I said to Quickel and then glanced over to Trooper Guth. Guth nodded without a word.

I then passed the affidavit across the table to Quickel. He read it over, nodded. "Yep. It's all true," he said as he leaned forward with the pen.

"Please note that this is being sworn under penalty of perjury," I said.

"Yes. I know," he said, signing his name on the bottom of the form.

Patrick Burns

With his biggest smile of the night, thinking this interview was finished and he had fooled us, Quickel placed both hands on the kitchen table for leverage as he stood up.

Halfway to his feet, I interrupted him.

"I just have one more thing to do."

Still standing halfway to his feet, bent over, frozen, with dismay now appearing on his face, he asked, "What now?"

"Now, now I'm going to arrest you!"

His look of dismay turned to shock and terror. "What, what do you mean, arrest me?"

"All these guns you swore were in your possession in April have been sitting in an FBI vault for the last year. Your story is an impossible lie. And I can prove it."

His face turned pale. "Wait, wait a minute. Just wait. Can I tell you the truth NOW?"

"Yes, you can," I said.

Corporal Guth slammed a photo array onto the kitchen table.

"Who hired you to buy the guns?" he demanded in a raised voice, no longer concealing his anger. His patience had run out.

"Him! That's him. He hired me!" Quickel blurted out. His nervousness now bordering on fear, he rushed to place his index finger on the image in the center of the six-photo line–up. It was a small Russian man with a boyish face, none other than Ivan Teleguz.

15   *What If I Tell You About a Murder?*

By the end of our interview with Quickel, he'd come clean and described every single gun purchase he made at the local gun shops.

Each purchase was at the direction of Ivan Teleguz. Each gun was selected by Teleguz, and Quickel filed the false ATF purchase record. Quickel was paid $100 for each transaction, money used to help fund his drug habit.

I now had enough evidence to charge Quickel with thirteen counts of filing false ATF forms 4473. Each violation was punishable for up to five years. He also lied under oath during the interview, exposing himself to another five years in federal prison.

Teleguz was also facing a very lengthy potential prison sentence for conspiracy to file false ATF forms and delivering the weapons across state lines from Pennsylvania to Massachusetts.

Along with those two, I still had their partner, Aleksei Safanov, sitting on ice. He was still in a county jail cell, facing local gun charges. But that was about to change.

It was time to break the news to Aleksei. The good news for him would be he would no longer face local charges. The bad news for him was he was about to face federal charges carrying a sentence of twenty years in prison.

I looked forward to breaking the news to him.

*****

The federal courthouse and ATF office are in downtown Springfield.

The county jail sits in a rural town on the outskirts of the city. I'd already called ahead to ask the guards to have the prisoner ready for my arrival. The beige two-story building is surrounded by twelve-foot high cement walls, barbed wire, and heavily wooded acres.

I pulled up to the gate of the first of a series of gates. The uniformed officer inspected my ATF badge and then looked up to another guard in a tower. The guard at the entrance gave the other a nod. Instantly, there's the sound of a click followed by the hum of a motor. Slowly, the large gate retracted in front of my car.

I pulled forward into the next lock. The large gate I just passed now closed behind me. Parked, locked between two twenty-foot razor-wire-topped gates, I go through the same process with the next set of guards. The new guards have a German Shepherd with them. The dog sniffs my car's tires. After the inspection, the guard waves me to move forward as the next gate opens in front of me.

Patrick Burns

A "TRANSFER DOCK" sign hangs over a steel door. I park next to it and go inside. Safanov is inside, handcuffed to a holding rail, sitting inside a small, temporary cell.

"Who are you?" he asks, looking up.

"Stand up. Turn around. Put your hands behind your back."

I handcuff him and take his arm. I thank the guards for their assistance and escort Safanov to my car.

"Who are you? Where do you think you are taking me?" He questions me while sitting in the back seat of my car as we head downtown. The preferred method to transport a prisoner would be with another officer assisting. But since I was still working solo from the ATF office, I often improvised.

"I'm a Special Agent with ATF. We're going to the courthouse."

"ATF? What is "ATF"?

"Alcohol, Tobacco, and Firearms."

"You are a cigarette investigator?" He laughs. "You investigate tobacco and vodka? Are you an idiot?"

"I'm arresting you for firearms violations."

"You can't, you fool. That would be double jeopardy. It's not allowed. Don't they teach you anything in cigarette school? I'm already in jail for a firearm charge. You can't charge me again. You people are all fools."

"We'll see about that."

"Yeah. You will see me walk out of here next week. Having an unregistered firearm is a penalty of 30 days and a fine. That's it!"

Within twenty minutes, we arrive at the courthouse. I wave to the guard, who then opens the garage door to the underground parking. The U.S. Marshals office is on the fourth floor.

Minutes later, we park near the elevators. "Let's go," I say as I pull him from the back seat of the car.

We arrived on the fourth floor. Still holding Safanov with one hand, I press the buzzer next to the door for the U.S. Marshals office.

"These guys will be taking you to see the judge later today," I advise him with a dollop of pleasure. "After you're convicted, they'll deliver you to Leavenworth Federal Prison, where you'll be spending the rest of your life."

The U.S. Marshals will take him from here. Moments later, as he's standing inside his cell, he calls out to the two Deputies standing nearby.

Patrick Burns

"Hey, you, cop," he says, face pressed up against the bars.

"What is it, Safanov?" a deputy asked.

"What the hell is that ATF guy talking about? Life in prison?"

"You're fucked, pal. I've seen the charges he's got against you. He's telling you the truth," the deputy replied as he turned his attention back to the TV monitor hung on the wall.

"Hey! I'm talking to you! I'm only supposed to do 30 days for the state gun charge. This is a mistake!"

"That charge has been dropped. You're now only facing federal charges. And like the ATF guy told you, you're going away for good."

"Fuck that! And fuck that ATF agent. What if I could tell you about a murder? I want to make a deal!"

16   *Ivan Did It*

Tough guy Safanov instantly became whining bitch rat Safanov. Once the reality hit that he'd be spending the next twenty-plus years in federal prison with no chance of parole kicked in, his attitude changed.

Soon after Safanov sang like a Russian canary, Corporal Guth's phone rang at the Lancaster PA State Police office.

"Hello? Corporal Guth."

"Ray. This is Detective Whitfield from Harrisonburg P.D. How are you doing?"

"Good. Good. What can I do for you? Do you have something new on the Sipe murder?"

"Do you know if one of Teleguz's guys lives near the county jail, on East King Street?"

"I might. I'd need to check the file."

"ATF grabbed a guy in Springfield, one of Ivan's crew. He says he wants to cooperate for a deal. He told the Deputies that a black man in Ivan's crew, who lived on East King Street, was the guy who killed Stephanie Sipe."

Guth flips through his folder and stops at a listing for one of Teleguz's crew.

"Here it is. East King Street under the name of Edwin Gilkes."

"Edwin Gilkes. I think that's our guy. Do you want me to pick him up? It looks like he's got an outstanding warrant for shoplifting. Okay. I'll pick him up."

*****

When I made the original case on Safanov for the AK-47 with an obliterated serial number, I got my foot in the door with Rick Winfield's Russian Task Force. After I put together arrest packages on Quickel and Ivan Teleguz, I got my full membership on the team. The two investigations were united.

That meant we would work hand-in-hand going forward. As a first step, Winfield assigned one of his Task Force officers, Don Brown, to join me on my next trip.

We were soon on our way to the East King Street Jail to interview Gilkes.

It was another full day of driving from Springfield, Massachusetts, to Lancaster. Again I took the route via Route 95 South, passing through New York City, then New Jersey, and then through countless miles of rural areas and mountains. Descending one winding mountain road, we saw cornfields. We were getting close to our destination.

Following the directions on my GPS, we eventually made our way to a dilapidated, older section of town. Halfway down the city street—surrounded by low-income housing and low-end commercial buildings, bails bondsmen, liquor shops, etc., —we spot the front entrance for the East King Street County Jail.

Once inside the facility, it is a circular layout. All the individual jail cells, toilets, showers, and small sitting areas surround a circular room filled with metal tables and chairs bolted to the floor. Behind a thick bulletproof glass window, guards have a clear view of it all.

The eyes in the building are watching us as we arrive and sit down with Gilkes. He's waiting for us, seated at one of the metal tables in the center. News of our visit won't take long to get back to Ivan. But there's no other option.

"Hi Edwin, I'm Patrick Burns, a Special Agent with ATF. This is Task Force Officer Don Brown. We have a few questions for you," I said, showing him our badges.

"Why do you want to talk to me? I didn't do nuthin' I'm just a thief."

"Is that so?" I said. "Well, that's not what we've been told."

Patrick Burns

"It's the truth. You ask anybody."

"Well," Brown asked. "Do you know Aleksey Safanov?"

"Sure. I know him."

"Well," I said, "he says, three years ago, you killed a young woman named Stephanie Sipe in her Harrisonburg, Virginia apartment."

"I ain't never killed nobody. Check my records!"

"Well, that's not what Safanov said," Brown came back. "He said you killed her. Aleksei is in jail right now. He's cooperating. He's looking for a deal. And he gave you up for the murder!"

"Look, man. What if I did know who killed her?"

"Okay," I said. "Who killed her?"

"I don't know for sure. But it might have been my roommate."

"Who was that?" I asked right away.

"Mike Hetrick."

Brown asked: "Why do you think he killed Stephanie?"

"Well, one night, around the time when she was killed, he came home with a cut on his hand."

"You think we believe that story?" I gave him a dubious look.

"It's true. I swear. Listen, the next day, a guy we know, Ivan, came over and took Mike to the emergency room. And the next time I saw Mike, he's got lots of cash. I think Ivan gave him $2,000 to kill her. Mike bought a stereo for our apartment with some of the cash."

"How do you know Ivan?" Brown asked. "You are talking about Ivan Teleguz? Right?"

"Yes. Ivan Teleguz, man. Mike and I did work for him; helped him sell guns and drugs too. But I ain't never done no murder. No way!"

Brown showed Gilkes a photo of Teleguz. "Show me the man that hired you to help traffic guns and drugs."

"That's him. That's Ivan!" Correctly identifying Ivan Teleguz.

Bingo, I think. Ironclad case.

Gilkes gives us everything we need to corroborate the testimony of Michael Quickel. Ivan Teleguz is the mastermind behind the gun and drug trafficking and the murder of Stephanie Sipe. Our meeting is over and highly successful.

But word has gotten out.

Patrick Burns

*****

Soon afterward, thousands of miles away in Vancouver, Washington, the future looks bright for a happy young couple as the soon-to-be bride and groom chat with her parents.

"Again, I want to say welcome to the family, son. We couldn't be happier or more proud. I know you'll make our daughter very happy."

"I'll do my best," the young Russian says with a charming smile.

Her mother agrees. "Ever since you met our Mary through the church group, I've never seen her so happy!"

"I love you guys, too," Teleguz replies. "By the way, I'd like to borrow your car to pick Mary up at the high school later today when she finishes her class. I want to go shopping for wedding rings."

"Of course, son." Mary's father hands Teleguz his car keys with a broad smile.

"Thanks, dad. And thanks for allowing me to live here until the wedding. We can save for our future."

The naïve family has no idea they are in the presence of a cold-blooded killer. They have no clue what happened to the last girl who wanted to marry their prospective son-in-law. The entire group—beaming smiles, glowing looks, enchanted in the joyful moment—has no idea how soon things will come crashing down.

Or how lucky they are it did.

*****

Back on the east coast, in the Harrisonburg P.D., Whitfield sits across a table from his new murder suspect, Michael Hetrick. Set on top of the table between them are a search warrant and a jar containing cotton swabs.

"Michael, I have a warrant for your DNA. Take a look at it. It includes the testimony of Alex Safanov and Edwin Gilkes. They both gave you up. They say you killed a young woman named Stephanie Sipe in 2001. This DNA sample will tell us if it was your blood on the murder weapon. And if it is your blood, you're going to be arrested. And the punishment for murder in Virginia is the death penalty."

Hetrick reads the affidavits. Sweat ran down his face, his hands shook. Occasionally, he glanced up at the detective. Finally, he looked up at the camera hanging in the corner of the room, recording the entire process.

Sensing that Hetrick has read the charges, Whitfield removes a swab from the jar on the table. He gestures for Hetrick to open his mouth.

Patrick Burns

But Hetrick keeps his mouth closed and stares blankly at the detective.

"Let's go. Open," Whitfield ordered as he leaned forward, aiming the swab at Hetrick's mouth.

Whitfield paused.

"Wait... We don't need to do that," Hetrick said finally.

"Why is that?"

"You're right. It is my blood on the knife."

"Stand up. Put your hands behind your back. You're under arrest for the murder of Stephanie Sipe."

"But I want to cooperate!"

"Oh? How's that?"

"I want to tell you who hired me. I was hired to do it."

"Okay, so who hired you? I'm listening."

"Ivan Teleguz hired me to kill her. And he hired Edwin to be a lookout. Ivan was mad that the woman forced him to pay child support. Edwin Gilkes was with me. He was part of it, the lookout. He stayed outside when I went in to kill her. But it was Ivan behind it all."

Whitfield jotted down his notes as the CCTV cameral recorded the confession.

"Anything else you can tell me about this?"

"He told me to give her a message when I slit her throat. He wanted her to know it was him who sent me."

"What was the message?"

"He told me to say, Ivan sent me."

Detective Whitfield put down his pen and looked up at the CCTV camera. As he did, he ran his finger across his neck, gesturing they could now cut off the recording. Case closed.

*****

In Springfield, the FBI building's parking spaces were filling up quickly as a caravan of dark-colored SUVs, assorted sedans, and marked police cars rushed in.

All headed to the rear portion of the lot behind the building. Energy levels were high. Adrenaline was building. Scores of heavily armed men and women, some clad in body armors, got out of the cars.

Inside the FBI office, RAC. Mike O'Reilly stood at his window, staring down as the troops arrived. Several marked units in the lot below him were from Springfield P.D. A couple of cruisers were from the west side. Two Massachusetts State Trooper K-9 handlers, dressed in their military-style blue uniforms, stand close to their vehicles chatting, sipping coffees. Their dog partners stretch their legs and relieve themselves in the open parking lot.

With a little delay, the small platoon of warriors made their way to the front entrance of the unsigned, gray, four-story commercial building. After climbing a staircase to the second floor, each group was buzzed in the security door entrance.

Some glanced up and waved to the overhead CCTV camera. Once inside, the receptionist directed them to the conference room. A large stash of bagels, donuts, coffee, and Danish was laid out in front of the conference room.

"Come on in, ladies and gentlemen." FBI Special Agent Winfield said with a smile, waving them in.

RAC Mike O'Reilly, and the soft-spoken, mild-mannered AUSA, Kevin O'Regan, watched the group attack the goodies and gather around.

Whiteboards—each with a hand-drawn diagram of a specific target location—hung on one wall. Each map listed the location of each of the target businesses and residences.

The details highlighted surrounding city streets, landmarks, and individuals expected to be at the places. Finally, the maps indicate where each assigned response team would set up and deploy when the green light is given.

Another agent walked around the room, mingling between the teams, as he passed out assignment booklets. Each has photographs of locations, targets, and intelligence information, such as whether weapons or innocent civilians might be present, etc.

"Arrest Team number one will take down Roman Zhirnov," Winfield said. "I'll be the team leader on Arrest Team one. Team member assignments are listed on each whiteboard and the front cover of the team booklets Officer Brown is passing out.

"We expect Zhirnov to be at the Russian Book Store. An officer from Springfield P.D. is on the scene now, doing surveillance. The Greek will inform us when Zhirnov arrives.

"Please note, Zhirnov is armed and extremely dangerous. Respond accordingly," pausing for a moment to let the caution set in. "Okay. After we make the arrest, Search Team One will search the location.

"Security Team One will also set up a "close" perimeter around the bookstore.

"We have an arrest warrant for Andrey Buynovskiy. Arrest Team Two will take him at his work location, the North End Body Shop. Once he's locked down, Search Team Two will search of the body shop."

Patrick Burns

Winfield goes over the team assignments and locations for security teams and other formalities and then turns to out-of-state targets.

"Pennsylvania State Police and ATF will pick up Quickel down in Lancaster."

"What about Ivan Teleguz?" one officer asked.

"Ivan Teleguz, for the moment, is in the wind. He evidently got tipped off. It's likely, we think, Edwin Gilkes got word to him, maybe out of fear. Or maybe one of the other prisoners at the East King Street Jail saw Gilkes being questioned and got word to him. Anyway, Telezguz has fled. But we'll find him soon enough."

*****

In Lancaster, Corporal Guth, and several ATF agents met at the State Police outpost to go over their own briefing.

"As soon as we get the word from FBI in Springfield," Guth said, "our arrest team will move in and take Quickel into custody. He'll then be brought to the U.S. Marshals office for processing.

*****

In Harrisonburg, VA, Detective Whitfield is busy at his desk, typing up a fugitive arrest warrant for Ivan Teleguz for the murder of Stephanie Sipe.

In Springfield, the raids begin.

First, we hit the bookstore. Roman Zhirnov, the former Russian soldier, turned American gun trafficker, was arrested without incident. He's taken away in handcuffs and marched down the sidewalk on the west side as curious pedestrians look on. News crews arrive shortly and begin coverage. While he is taken away, the search starts at the bookstore.

Simultaneously, the raid began at the Body Shop. Andrey Buynovskiy, a large, lumpy, sort of Neanderthal-looking thug, is taken down to the pavement and placed in handcuffs. He's put into a police car and taken to the U.S. Marshals' Office for prints and processing.

Quickel is taken into custody at his apartment by Corporal Guth and a team of ATF agents. They also visit the local gun shops to conduct interviews and obtain additional records.

*****

While arrests of his accomplices go down on the east coast, Teleguz remains free. The sun is bright. It's a beautiful day in Vancouver, and the future couldn't look any more promising. He's safely thousands of miles away, ready to start his new life with a pretty and unsuspecting bride.

****

Seated in his office, Corporal Guth picked up the telephone and dialed my ATF office in Springfield.

Patrick Burns

"Agent Burns, I think I might know where we can find Ivan Teleguz."

Soon afterward, I send an arrest warrant to our Vancouver ATF office.

*****

As Teleguz drove his future father-in-law's car toward the front of the high school, he saw Mary, his young bride-to-be, up ahead. She smiled and waved while standing on the sidewalk. She had no idea her world is about to come crashing down.

As Teleguz waved back, a dark-colored SUV screeched to a stop in front of his car, parking sideways across the road, blocking his path.

Ivan slammed on the brakes. "What the fuck?"

He looked into his rearview mirror. "Fuck!" he mumbled as he sees another SUV up against his rear bumper. He was blocked in. As he turned forward to the sound of car doors opening, he sees a half-dozen men, all wearing blue ATF raid jackets, swarming around his car.

There were two at each of his doors. All had their guns pointed directly at his head.

"Hands up, motherfucker!" one agent shouted. "Get out!"

Teleguz hesitantly rolled down the window. "Officers, this must be a mistake," he said with a charming, boyish smile, "I'm on my way to pick up my fiancée. She's at the high school."

The agent standing next to the driver's side door said nothing. He simply yanked opened the door, grabbed Ivan by the collar, and threw him to the pavement. Looking down at the killer, one foot on his neck, the agent smiled.

"The wedding is canceled."

On July 1, 2004, three years after the murder of Stephanie Sipe, Ivan Teleguz was arrested. He was returned to Virginia where he was indicted by a Rockingham County grand jury for the willful and premeditated murder of another person, by another person for hire, as an accessory before the fact, in violation of Virginia Criminal Code 18.231(2)

During the four-day trial, the medical examiner testified that Stephanie suffered many cuts and wounds. He described some as defensive wounds. He also detailed her other injuries.

One stab wound extended from her neck on the left side of her head straight through to the right side of her neck. It sliced open her windpipe and esophagus. Stephanie also suffered a third fatal wound. Approximately two and one-half inches deep, it severed her trachea, larynx, and a major artery.

In Springfield Federal Court, Teleguz was also charged with conspiracy to deal firearms without a license and to possess firearms with obliterated serial numbers, in violation of Federal Codes, 18 U.S.C. sections 371, 922(a)(1)(A), and 922(k).☐

His co-defendants, Aleksei Safanov, Roman Zhirnov, Andrey Buynovskiy, and Michael Quickel, all pled guilty. During the trial, Quickel testified against Teleguz.

Regarding the gun trafficking charges, the federal jury convicted Teleguz on all counts. The district court judge sentenced Teleguz to fifty-one months in federal prison, followed by three years of supervised release.

For their testimony against Teleguz, Michael Hetrick and Edwin Gilkes received reduced sentences for their roles in the murder. Gilkes received a 15-year sentence, and Hetrick was sentenced to life in prison.

In Virginia, the state jury also found Teleguz guilty for the murder of Stephanie Sipe. He was sentenced to death by lethal injection.

Unfortunately, in 2017, right before the death penalty was about to be imposed, the Governor of Virginia commuted Teleguz's death sentence to life in prison without parole.

Fortunately, El Loco, the wannabe cop-killer, remains dead as of the printing of this book.

*****

FBI Special Agent Rick Winfield continued on the job and was later put in charge of the FBI's terrorism cases. He eventually developed terrific interagency relationships and even took down his "Someone Talked" poster.

Corporal Raymond Guth of the Pennsylvania State Police was promoted to Sergeant.

Corporal Sean Condon, AKA "Hutch," was promoted to Sergeant.

Patrick Burns

Norman Shink, or "Starsky," finished his career with the Massachusetts State Police.

AUSA Paul Smyth was appointed to be a federal judge.

AUSA Kevin O'Regan later retired

I was transferred to the FBI's new, top-secret anti-terrorist unit. We were housed in a fortified location hidden beneath a parking lot on the Marine Corps Base at Quantico, VA.

While working there, I identified and investigated terrorist networks supplying Improvised Explosive Devices (I.E.D.) components to al-Qaeda in Iraq and Afghanistan. Eventually, this led me to conducting terrorist investigations from the Forward Operating Base in Mosul, Iraq. After troop withdrawals began and we pulled out of Mosul, it became part of the ISIS Caliphate.

On my last day on the job with ATF, the last piece of government equipment I needed to turn in was my car. I had been assigned several vehicles over the years. Each time I was issued a new vehicle, I would transfer everything from the old car's trunk to the new vehicle.

The "everything" included all of my tactical gear and one stuffed toy, the toy my son Patrick had tossed into my car on one of my first days on the job in Springfield. He'd put it there to go in his place on the arrest operation, a good luck charm.

Ivan Sent Me

When I turned in my car that last day, I reached deep inside the trunk and grabbed the stuffed toy turtle.

When I retired, so too did the turtle.

Patrick Burns, U. S. Special Agent (Ret.), spent over twenty years in Federal Law Enforcement, conducting hundreds of investigations, including cases against some of the world's most sophisticated and dangerous criminals and terrorists.

Whether the work required tedious records analysis, innovative interview tactics, actual car chases, foot chases, gunfights, or pursuits throughout America, the Middle East, or Europe, most of his investigations ended in successful captures and convictions.

The events and characters portrayed here are real; a glimpse into a U.S. federal agent's real-life work. His first non-fiction book, *The Coin Store: A True Story of Drug Cartels, Mobsters, Cops, and Agents,* has sold thousands of copies worldwide. He is now retired and living abroad and continues writing.

JEBWizard Publishing offers a hybrid approach to publishing. By taking a vested interest in your book's success, we put our reputation on the line to create and market a quality publication. We offer a customized solution based on your individual project needs.

Our authors' catalog spans the spectrum of fiction, non-fiction, Young Adult, True Crime, Self-help, and Children's books.

Contact us for submission guidelines at

https://www.jebwizardpublishing.com

Info@jebwizardpublishing.com

Or in writing at

JEBWizard Publishing

37 Park Forest Rd.

Cranston, RI 02920

Made in the USA
Monee, IL
07 July 2026

56550194R10144